The Huge Book of Intriguing Facts

by
Jake Jacobs

* * * * *

Published by Jake Jacobs

1.

The black-footed ferret (Mustela nigripes) is one of the most endangered mammals in North America.

2.

They are native to the Great Plains of North America and were once widely distributed across the grasslands.

3.

Black-footed ferrets are small carnivores, measuring around 18 to 24 inches in length, with a tail length of 5 to 6 inches.

4.

They have a slender body, short legs, and a black mask around their eyes, giving them a distinctive appearance.

5.

Black-footed ferrets are nocturnal animals, meaning they are most active during the night.

6.

Their primary diet consists of prairie dogs, which make up around 90% of their food source.

7.

They are highly specialized predators and have developed adaptations, such as a slender body and sharp teeth, to help them catch and consume prairie dogs.

8.

Black-footed ferrets are solitary animals and prefer to live alone, except during the breeding season.

9.

They are territorial and mark their territories with scent markings.

10.

The black-footed ferret population drastically declined due to habitat loss, disease, and the decline of prairie dog populations.

11.

In 1981, the black-footed ferret was thought to be extinct until a small population was discovered in Wyoming.

12.

Efforts were made to breed and reintroduce black-footed ferrets into the wild to help restore their population.

13.

The captive breeding program has been successful, and reintroduction efforts have resulted in the establishment of new populations in several states.

14.

Black-footed ferrets have a lifespan of around 3 to 4 years in the wild but can live up to 9 years in captivity.

15.

They are highly adapted to living in underground burrows, which they use for shelter and to raise their young.

16.

The black-footed ferret is a member of the Mustelidae family, which also includes other carnivorous mammals like weasels, otters, and badgers.

17.

They have a keen sense of smell, which helps them locate prey and navigate their environment.

18.

Black-footed ferrets are agile climbers and can scale trees and rocks with ease.

19.

They have a specialized tooth structure that allows them to deliver a lethal bite to their prey, targeting the vital organs.

20.

Black-footed ferrets are known for their distinctive vocalizations, including barks, chuckles, and hisses.

21.

The black-footed ferret is listed as endangered under the Endangered Species Act.

22.

They are the only ferret species native to North America.

23.

Black-footed ferrets have a unique body shape with a long, slender neck and a slim, elongated body.

24.

They have excellent hearing and can detect sounds of prey even when underground.

25.

Black-footed ferrets are highly elusive animals and are difficult to spot in the wild.

26.

They have a natural immunity to the venom of prairie rattlesnakes, which allows them to prey on the snakes without being harmed.

27.

Black-footed ferrets are crepuscular, meaning they are most active during dawn and dusk.

28.

They have a keen sense of balance and are adept at maneuvering through complex underground burrow systems.

29.

Black-footed ferrets are known to exhibit playful behavior, engaging in activities such as chasing, wrestling, and pouncing.

30.

They have a unique fur pattern, with a mixture of brown, black, and white markings, providing effective camouflage in their grassland habitat.

31.

The black-footed ferret's scientific name, Mustela nigripes, translates to "black-footed weasel."

32.

They have sharp retractable claws that help them dig burrows and capture prey.

33.

Black-footed ferrets are opportunistic hunters and will consume other small mammals if prairie dogs are not readily available.

34.

They are excellent swimmers and can traverse water bodies with
ease.

35.

Black-footed ferrets communicate through a variety of vocalizations,
body postures, and scent markings.

36.

They have a high metabolic rate and require a diet high in protein to
sustain their energy levels.

37.

Black-footed ferrets are known for their ability to squeeze through
tight spaces due to their flexible bodies.

38.

They have a specialized digestive system that allows them to
efficiently process and extract nutrients from their prey.

39.

Black-footed ferrets are highly territorial and will defend their home
range from other individuals.

40.

They have a gestation period of around 42 to 45 days and give birth
to litters of 3 to 5 kits.

41.

Black-footed ferret kits are born blind and helpless and rely on their
mother for nourishment and protection.

42.

They have a strong sense of curiosity and will investigate their
surroundings, often poking their heads out of burrow entrances to
observe their surroundings.

43.

Black-footed ferrets have a hierarchical social structure, with
dominant individuals asserting control over resources and territories.

44.

They are efficient hunters and can consume a prairie dog within
minutes, leaving little to no remains.

45.

Black-footed ferrets have been the focus of conservation efforts to
restore their populations and preserve their natural habitat.

46.

They are capable of running at high speeds, reaching up to 15 miles
per hour.

47.

Black-footed ferrets are adept at climbing in and out of burrow
entrances, often using their forelimbs to pull themselves up.

48.

They have a keen sense of spatial awareness and can navigate
through intricate tunnel systems without getting lost.

49.

Black-footed ferrets have large, round eyes that provide them with
excellent vision in low-light conditions.

50.

They are known for their war dance behavior, where they perform a series of sideways hops and twists to confuse and disorient their prey.

51.

The black house spider (Badumna insignis) is a species of spider native to Australia.

52.

They are commonly found in urban areas, including houses, sheds, and other man-made structures.

53.

Black house spiders belong to the family Desidae, which includes over 500 species.

54.

The females are larger than the males, measuring around 1.5 to 2 centimeters in body length.

55.

They have a dark brown to black coloration, hence the name "black house spider."

56.

Black house spiders are known for their strong, irregular webs, which they use to capture prey.

57.

They typically build their webs in dark, sheltered locations, such as corners, crevices, and under eaves.

58.

The webs are sticky and entangle flying insects, providing the spider with a reliable food source.

59.

Despite their intimidating appearance, black house spiders are not aggressive towards humans and prefer to avoid contact.

60.

They have venomous fangs and can deliver a bite if provoked, but their venom is not considered medically significant to humans.

61.

Black house spiders are solitary creatures and usually live alone, except during the mating season.

62.

Males are known to wander in search of mates, often entering houses and other structures.

63.

The lifespan of a black house spider is around 2 to 3 years.

64.

They undergo molting to grow, shedding their exoskeleton and emerging with a larger size.

65.

Black house spiders are adept climbers and can move quickly across vertical surfaces.

66.

They have eight legs, which they use to navigate their web and capture prey.

67.

Their diet primarily consists of insects, including flies, mosquitoes, moths, and other small arthropods.

68.

Female black house spiders are responsible for producing egg sacs that contain numerous eggs.

69.

The egg sacs are protected within the web and guarded by the female until the spiderlings hatch.

70.

Spiderlings undergo several molts before reaching maturity.

71.

Black house spiders play a role in controlling insect populations, acting as natural pest controllers.

72.

They are not known to cause structural damage to buildings, despite their presence in man-made structures.

73.

Black house spiders are often mistaken for funnel-web spiders due to their similar appearance, but they are not as venomous.

74.

They are resilient to various environmental conditions and can survive in both urban and natural habitats.

75.

Black house spiders are sensitive to vibrations and movements in their web, enabling them to detect potential prey.

76.

They are nocturnal hunters, primarily active during the night.

77.

In some cases, black house spiders may build their webs near outdoor lights to attract insects.

78.

They have specialized sensory organs called "slit sense organs" on their legs, which detect vibrations.

79.

Black house spiders are capable of regenerating lost legs if they are damaged or severed.

80.

They have a unique method of capturing prey, using their fangs to deliver a paralyzing bite before wrapping the prey in silk.

81.

Black house spiders are known to eat their old web and rebuild it, recycling the silk protein to create a new web.

82.

They are sensitive to changes in temperature and humidity, often adjusting their web-building behavior accordingly.

83.

Black house spiders have multiple eyes arranged in two rows, providing them with a wide field of vision.

84.

They are not known for their ability to jump but can move quickly using their legs.

85.

While black house spiders are not commonly kept as pets, some individuals may choose to observe them in captivity.

86.

They have a mild, non-aggressive temperament, making them relatively easy to handle if necessary.

87.

Black house spiders contribute to the ecological balance by preying on insects that may be considered pests.

88.

They are beneficial to gardens and agricultural areas by helping to control pest populations naturally.

89.

Black house spiders have been studied for their silk production, which has potential applications in various industries.

90.

They are considered part of the natural biodiversity of Australia and play a role in the local ecosystem.

91.

The mating behavior of black house spiders involves intricate courtship rituals performed by the male to attract a female.

92.

The female may lay multiple egg sacs throughout her lifetime, each containing dozens of eggs.

93.

Black house spiders are susceptible to predation by birds, lizards, and other insectivorous animals.

94.

They are not typically aggressive towards other spiders unless competing for resources or defending their territory.

95.

The silk produced by black house spiders is known for its strength and elasticity.

96.

They have been observed building their webs in close proximity to each other, forming clusters of interconnected webs.

97.

Black house spiders have a cryptic coloration, blending well with their surroundings to avoid detection by predators.

98.

They are generally considered harmless to humans, and their presence should be tolerated as a natural part of the environment.

99.

Black house spiders are adapted to survive in diverse climatic conditions, ranging from arid regions to more humid environments.

100.

Their silk has been used in scientific research, particularly in the development of biomaterials and nanotechnology.

101.

The Murray Springs Clovis Site is an archaeological site located in southeastern Arizona, USA.

102.

It is considered one of the most significant Clovis culture sites in North America.

103.

The site was discovered in the 1960s by Charles Stearns and Ray Fraser during a survey of potential dam sites.

104.

It is named after the Murray family, who owned the land where the site is located.

105.

The site dates back approximately 13,000 years and provides important insights into the early human occupation of the Americas.

106.

Archaeologists have unearthed numerous Clovis artifacts at the site, including stone tools, spear points, and bone fragments.

107.

The spear points found at Murray Springs are distinctive with their fluted design, which is characteristic of the Clovis culture.

108.

The site's excavation has provided evidence of early Paleoindian hunting and butchering practices.

109.

The remains of extinct megafauna, such as mammoths and horses, have been found at the site, indicating the presence of large game in the region.

110.

Murray Springs is believed to have been a hunting camp where Clovis people utilized the natural resources of the area.

111.

The site is situated near a natural spring, which would have provided a reliable water source for the inhabitants.

112.

Excavations at Murray Springs have also revealed evidence of hearths and fire pits used by the Clovis people.

113.

The site's stratigraphy, or layers of soil and sediment, have helped archaeologists reconstruct the history of human occupation over time.

114.

Murray Springs has been extensively studied and researched by archaeologists, contributing to our understanding of early human migration and settlement patterns.

115.

The site's proximity to other Clovis culture sites in the region suggests a larger network of human populations during the time period.

116.

The artifacts found at Murray Springs provide important clues about the technology, craftsmanship, and resource exploitation of the Clovis people.

117.

The discovery of bison bones with distinctive butchering marks suggests that the Clovis people were skilled hunters and utilized all parts of the animal.

118.

The presence of ancient tools made from materials like chert and obsidian indicates long-distance trade and resource procurement.

119.

Murray Springs is located in the San Pedro River valley, a region that would have provided diverse ecological resources for the Clovis people.

120.

The site's archaeological significance led to its inclusion in the National Register of Historic Places in 1966.

121.

The excavation and research at Murray Springs have provided valuable data for studying the peopling of the Americas and the Clovis culture.

122.

The site has helped support the theory that the Clovis people were among the first to colonize North America.

123.

Murray Springs has yielded evidence of multiple occupation episodes, indicating the site was used by different groups over time.

124.

The artifacts found at the site have been carefully cataloged, analyzed, and preserved for future research.

125.

The study of Murray Springs has contributed to our understanding of prehistoric human adaptations to changing environments.

126.

The site has served as a training ground for archaeology students and professionals, offering hands-on experience in excavation techniques.

127.

Murray Springs has also been used for public outreach and education, allowing visitors to learn about the region's prehistory and archaeology.

128.

The site's location in a picturesque landscape makes it an attractive destination for tourists and nature enthusiasts.

129.

Ongoing research at Murray Springs continues to shed light on the cultural practices, lifeways, and interactions of the Clovis people.

130.

The Clovis culture, represented by sites like Murray Springs, is considered a cornerstone of North American archaeology.

131.

The discoveries at Murray Springs have challenged previous assumptions about the timeline of human migration into the Americas.

132.

The site's archaeological investigations have been conducted using advanced scientific techniques, such as radiocarbon dating and DNA analysis.

133.

Murray Springs has provided evidence of the complexity and sophistication of Clovis tool-making techniques.

134.

The site has also yielded evidence of cultural continuity and change over thousands of years.

135.

Murray Springs has been an important case study in understanding the peopling of the New World and the earliest human adaptations to diverse environments.

136.

The preservation of the site's archaeological remains has been a collaborative effort involving federal, state, and local agencies.

137.

The study of Murray Springs has fostered collaborations between archaeologists, anthropologists, geologists, and other scientists.

138.

The site's excavation has required careful attention to detail, as even small artifacts and bone fragments can provide valuable insights.

139.

The discoveries at Murray Springs have raised questions about the social organization and mobility patterns of the Clovis people.

140.

The site has served as a benchmark for understanding the spread of the Clovis culture across different regions of North America.

141.

The archaeological investigations at Murray Springs have inspired further research into the early peopling of the Americas.

142.

The site's location near modern communities has sparked interest and engagement from local residents in the preservation and interpretation of the site.

143.

The artifacts found at Murray Springs are displayed in museums and educational institutions, allowing the public to appreciate their cultural and historical significance.

144.

The study of Murray Springs has contributed to the broader field of archaeology by refining dating techniques and methodologies.

145.

The site's excavation has been guided by ethical considerations, such as collaboration with Native American tribes and respect for cultural heritage.

146.

The research at Murray Springs has generated scholarly publications, contributing to the body of knowledge on the Clovis culture and early human history.

147.

The site's significance extends beyond the field of archaeology, as it provides insights into the deep history of the Americas.

148.

The discoveries at Murray Springs have sparked debates and discussions among archaeologists and anthropologists regarding human migration and cultural development.

149.

The site has been a source of inspiration for artists, writers, and filmmakers seeking to explore the rich history of the region.

150.

The ongoing study of Murray Springs demonstrates the importance of preserving and understanding our archaeological heritage for future generations.

151.

Old Oraibi is one of the oldest continuously inhabited settlements in North America.

152.

Located on the Hopi Indian Reservation in Arizona, USA, it is considered a sacred place by the Hopi people.

153.

The settlement is believed to have been established around the 11th century.

154.

Old Oraibi is situated on three mesas, with each mesa representing a different clan.

155.

The village is known for its adobe-style architecture, with multi-story buildings made from local materials.

156.

The layout of Old Oraibi follows traditional Hopi planning principles, with narrow, winding streets and interconnected homes.

157.

The community is built around a central plaza, which serves as a gathering place for ceremonies and social events.

158.

The Hopi people of Old Oraibi maintain a traditional way of life, practicing agriculture, pottery-making, and traditional arts and crafts.

159.

The village is known for its intricate pottery, featuring unique designs and symbolism.

160.

Old Oraibi is a spiritual center for the Hopi people, with sacred sites and kivas (underground ceremonial chambers) scattered throughout the village.

161.

The village has been a stronghold of Hopi culture and resistance, surviving centuries of colonization and attempts at assimilation.

162.

Old Oraibi is governed by a traditional Hopi council known as the Oraibi Traditional Council, which makes decisions based on Hopi customary law and traditions.

163.

The village has a strong sense of community, with close-knit families and a cooperative spirit among residents.

164.

Old Oraibi has a rich oral tradition, with stories and legends passed down through generations.

165.

The Hopi people of Old Oraibi are known for their dances and ceremonies, which are performed throughout the year to honor ancestors and maintain a harmonious relationship with the natural world.

166.

The village is surrounded by breathtaking desert landscapes, offering panoramic views of the mesas and canyons.

167.

Old Oraibi has been a subject of study and research for anthropologists and archaeologists interested in understanding indigenous cultures and their resilience.

168.

The village has witnessed significant historical events, including the arrival of Spanish missionaries and the establishment of the Hopi Reservation.

169.

Visitors to Old Oraibi are often welcomed to participate in traditional ceremonies and learn about Hopi culture and customs.

170.

The village serves as a cultural and educational center, offering workshops and programs on Hopi traditions and arts.

171.

Old Oraibi is known for its strong sense of spirituality, with a deep connection to the land and the cycles of nature.

172.

The village is home to renowned Hopi artists and craftsmen, who create beautiful jewelry, pottery, and artwork inspired by their cultural heritage.

173.

Old Oraibi has its own unique dialect of the Hopi language, reflecting the village's distinct identity and history.

174.

The Hopi people of Old Oraibi practice sustainable agriculture, using traditional farming techniques and embracing the principles of conservation.

175.

The village has faced challenges in recent years, including water scarcity and threats to traditional land rights.

176.

Old Oraibi has been a site of cultural exchange, with indigenous peoples from different tribes visiting the village to share knowledge and traditions.

177.

The village is a source of inspiration for artists, writers, and filmmakers seeking to capture the beauty and resilience of indigenous cultures.

178.

Old Oraibi has been recognized as a National Historic Landmark for its cultural and historical significance.

179.

The village has a vibrant arts and crafts market, where visitors can purchase authentic Hopi-made products directly from the artisans.

180.

Old Oraibi hosts annual festivals and events, showcasing traditional dances, music, and ceremonies.

181.

The village's architecture and construction techniques reflect the wisdom and ingenuity of the Hopi people, who have adapted to the harsh desert environment.

182.

Old Oraibi has a strong sense of intergenerational knowledge transfer, with elders playing a vital role in passing down traditions to younger generations.

183.

The village has a deep respect for the natural world, with rituals and ceremonies dedicated to maintaining balance and harmony with the Earth.

184.

Old Oraibi is a place of pilgrimage for many Hopi people, who come to reconnect with their ancestral roots and seek spiritual guidance.

185.

The village has inspired numerous scholarly studies and publications, contributing to the understanding of indigenous cultures and histories.

186.

Old Oraibi is known for its intricate sand paintings, created by skilled Hopi artists as a form of spiritual expression and healing.

187.

The village has been a gathering place for intertribal meetings and negotiations, serving as a hub for cultural exchange and diplomacy.

188.

Old Oraibi has its own unique calendar, based on the cycles of the moon and the agricultural seasons.

189.

The village is home to traditional Hopi farmers who cultivate corn, beans, squash, and other crops using age-old agricultural techniques.

190.

Old Oraibi has its own system of governance and dispute resolution, rooted in the values and traditions of the Hopi people.

191.

The village has been a site of resistance against encroachments on indigenous lands and attempts to erode Hopi cultural practices.

192.

Old Oraibi has a rich ceremonial life, with rituals marking important life events, such as birth, coming-of-age, marriage, and death.

193.

The village is known for its skilled weavers, who create intricate textiles and baskets using traditional techniques.

194.

Old Oraibi has a deep connection to the spiritual realm, with beliefs in ancestral spirits and a reverence for the unseen forces of the universe.

195.

The village has a strong sense of communal living, with shared responsibilities and a collective approach to decision-making.

196.

Old Oraibi has been a site of healing and spiritual renewal for those seeking solace and guidance.

197.

The village is known for its hospitality, with visitors welcomed as honored guests and given an opportunity to learn about Hopi culture.

198.

Old Oraibi has inspired the establishment of cultural centers and museums dedicated to preserving and promoting Hopi traditions.

199.

The village has faced challenges in preserving its cultural heritage in the face of modern influences and economic pressures.

200.

Old Oraibi remains a vibrant and thriving community, demonstrating the resilience and strength of the Hopi people in preserving their cultural identity and way of life.

201.

The Point of Pines Sites are a collection of prehistoric Native American ruins located in the Gila River Valley of Arizona, USA.

202.

The sites are part of the Hohokam culture, which existed from approximately 300 BCE to 1450 CE.

203.

The Point of Pines Sites are known for their well-preserved adobe and stone structures, including dwellings, ball courts, and ceremonial platforms.

204.

The sites span an area of approximately 45 acres and are divided into three main clusters: Casa Blanca, Pueblo del Arroyo, and Ventana.

205.

Casa Blanca is the largest cluster and contains the most extensive ruins, including large multi-room adobe structures.

206.

The architecture at Point of Pines Sites showcases the advanced construction techniques of the Hohokam, who built with mud plaster and used wooden beams for support.

207.

The ruins at Point of Pines Sites offer valuable insights into Hohokam social organization, including evidence of complex hierarchical structures.

208.

The sites were likely occupied by several hundred people at their peak, making them significant centers of Hohokam community life.

209.

Archaeological excavations have revealed artifacts such as pottery, stone tools, jewelry, and ceremonial objects, providing clues about Hohokam daily life and cultural practices.

210.

The Hohokam people of the Point of Pines Sites were skilled farmers and developed sophisticated irrigation systems to cultivate crops in the arid desert environment.

211.

Evidence suggests that the Hohokam grew crops such as corn, beans, squash, and cotton, contributing to their sustainable and prosperous way of life.

212.

The Hohokam at Point of Pines Sites traded with neighboring communities, exchanging goods and ideas across vast distances.

213.

The sites contain evidence of extensive trade networks, with artifacts from distant regions indicating long-distance travel and cultural exchange.

214.

The Hohokam were skilled artisans, creating intricately designed pottery with elaborate geometric patterns and stylized animal motifs.

215.

The Point of Pines Sites provide valuable information about Hohokam religious beliefs and ceremonial practices, including evidence of ritualistic offerings and burials.

216.

Excavations have uncovered petroglyphs and rock art, showcasing the Hohokam's artistic expression and connection to the natural world.

217.

The sites have been studied extensively by archaeologists, contributing to our understanding of the Hohokam culture and its contributions to Southwestern prehistory.

218.

Point of Pines Sites were inhabited for over a thousand years, showcasing the longevity and adaptability of the Hohokam people.

219.

The location of the sites in the Gila River Valley provided the Hohokam with a diverse and abundant natural environment, supporting their agricultural and hunting activities.

220.

The Point of Pines Sites are believed to have been abandoned around the 14th century, possibly due to changes in climate or social factors.

221.

The ruins have been protected and preserved by the Gila River Indian Community, who maintain a close connection to their ancestral lands.

222.

Point of Pines Sites have been listed on the National Register of Historic Places, recognizing their cultural and historical significance.

223.

The sites offer visitors a glimpse into the lives of the Hohokam people, with interpretive trails and signage providing educational opportunities.

224.

The Point of Pines Sites are an important cultural heritage site for Native American tribes, who continue to hold spiritual and cultural connections to the area.

225.

The ruins are a living testament to the ingenuity and resourcefulness of the Hohokam, who thrived in the desert landscape for centuries.

226.

The sites have been used as a backdrop for educational programs, allowing students and researchers to learn about archaeology and Native American history.

227.

Point of Pines Sites have inspired artwork, literature, and cultural expressions, serving as a source of inspiration for contemporary Native American artists.

228.

The preservation of the sites helps foster a sense of pride and identity among the Gila River Indian Community, reinforcing their cultural heritage and ancestral ties.

229.

The Point of Pines Sites continue to yield new discoveries and insights through ongoing archaeological research, expanding our knowledge of the Hohokam culture.

230.

The Hohokam people of the Point of Pines Sites were part of a larger network of ancient civilizations in the Southwest, with connections to cultures such as the Ancestral Puebloans and Mogollon.

231.

The sites offer a glimpse into the daily lives of the Hohokam, including their diet, housing, and social interactions.

232.

The Point of Pines Sites provide evidence of Hohokam textile production, with fragments of woven fabrics and tools used for weaving found in excavations.

233.

The sites contain evidence of defensive structures, suggesting the Hohokam faced occasional conflict and the need to protect their communities.

234.

Excavations at the Point of Pines Sites have revealed evidence of intentional remodeling and modifications to existing structures, indicating a dynamic and evolving society.

235.

The sites have served as gathering places for contemporary Native American communities, who come together to celebrate their culture, traditions, and ancestral connections.

236.

The Hohokam at Point of Pines Sites were skilled astronomers, using celestial observations to mark important agricultural and ceremonial events.

237.

The sites showcase the Hohokam's respect for the natural environment, with evidence of sustainable resource management and conservation practices.

238.

The Hohokam people at the Point of Pines Sites had a complex system of social organization, with specialized roles and responsibilities within the community.

239.

The sites are an important reminder of the rich cultural heritage that existed in the Southwest long before the arrival of Europeans.

240.

The Point of Pines Sites have served as a platform for community engagement and education, with local tribes and organizations collaborating on interpretive programs and cultural events.

241.

The sites contain evidence of Hohokam trade with Mesoamerican cultures, indicating a network of exchange that stretched from Central America to the Southwest.

242.

The ruins have been studied using advanced archaeological techniques, including ground-penetrating radar and 3D modeling, to better understand their spatial layout and architecture.

243.

The Point of Pines Sites have provided valuable insights into Hohokam burial practices, including evidence of cremation and inhumation.

244.

The Hohokam at Point of Pines Sites were skilled potters, creating vessels of various shapes and sizes for cooking, storage, and ceremonial purposes.

245.

The sites contain evidence of Hohokam agricultural terracing, a method of cultivating crops on sloping terrain to optimize water retention and soil fertility.

246.

The ruins have attracted visitors from around the world, drawn to the mystery and beauty of these ancient structures.

247.

The Point of Pines Sites have inspired scientific research on climate change and its impact on ancient societies, providing valuable data for understanding past environmental shifts.

248.

The sites offer opportunities for hands-on learning and archaeological fieldwork, allowing students and volunteers to participate in excavations and contribute to the preservation of cultural heritage.

249.

The Point of Pines Sites have been a source of pride and cultural identity for the Gila River Indian Community, who actively engage in their preservation and interpretation.

250.

The ruins stand as a testament to the resilience and ingenuity of the Hohokam people, who thrived in the challenging desert landscape and left behind a lasting legacy of cultural achievement.

251.

Edmund Randolph was born on August 10, 1753, in Williamsburg, Virginia, to a prominent colonial family.

252.

Randolph was the seventh Governor of Virginia, serving from 1786 to 1788.

253.

He played a significant role in the drafting and ratification of the
United States Constitution.

254.

Randolph was appointed as the first Attorney General of the United
States by President George Washington in 1789.

255.

He served as the Secretary of State under President Washington from
1794 to 1795.

256.

Randolph was known for his strong advocacy for states' rights and a
limited central government.

257.

He was an influential figure in the Virginia ratifying convention,
where he played a key role in securing Virginia's approval of the
Constitution.

258.

Randolph was a skilled lawyer and served as defense counsel in
many notable legal cases, including the defense of British soldiers
accused of the Boston Massacre.

259.

He was a member of the influential Virginia dynasty, which included
his cousin Thomas Jefferson and his brother-in-law Richard Bland
Lee.

260.

Randolph's father was a mentor to Thomas Jefferson and helped
foster Randolph's interest in law and politics.

261.

Randolph was instrumental in the creation of the Virginia Plan, which laid the foundation for the structure of the federal government.

262.

He proposed the "Randolph Resolutions" during the Constitutional Convention, advocating for a strong central government with a separation of powers.

263.

Randolph was one of the key architects of the system of checks and balances in the Constitution, ensuring a balance of power between the three branches of government.

264.

He was a proponent of individual rights and civil liberties, and his ideas influenced the development of the Bill of Rights.

265.

Randolph played a pivotal role in the drafting of the Judiciary Act of 1789, which established the federal court system.

266.

Despite his contributions to the federal government, Randolph resigned as Secretary of State due to disagreements with President Washington's policies.

267.

Randolph was involved in the controversial negotiations with France during the XYZ Affair, which strained relations between the two countries.

268.

He was known for his eloquent speaking and persuasive writing skills, making him a respected and influential figure in early American politics.

269.

Randolph was a vocal opponent of slavery and advocated for gradual emancipation and the colonization of freed slaves in Africa.

270.

He was one of the founders of the American Colonization Society, which sought to establish a colony in Africa for freed slaves.

271.

Randolph's political career was not without controversy. He was accused of accepting bribes during his time as Secretary of State but was ultimately cleared of any wrongdoing.

272.

Randolph was a supporter of the Federalist Party, but his disagreements with some of their policies led him to resign from President Washington's cabinet.

273.

He later became a prominent figure in the Democratic-Republican Party, aligning himself with Thomas Jefferson and James Madison.

274.

Randolph served as a delegate to the Virginia Ratifying Convention and played a crucial role in persuading Virginia to ratify the Constitution.

275.

He was a strong advocate for religious freedom and played a key role in the passage of the Virginia Statute for Religious Freedom.

276.

Randolph was a dedicated public servant and held numerous positions in Virginia government throughout his career, including serving as Attorney General and Governor.

277.

He was deeply committed to preserving the rights and liberties of the individual and believed in the importance of a written constitution.

278.

Randolph was an influential voice in shaping the concept of federalism, advocating for a balance of power between the national and state governments.

279.

He was a proponent of strong executive authority but also believed in the importance of legislative checks on the executive branch.

280.

Randolph's tenure as Governor of Virginia was marked by efforts to strengthen the state's economy and infrastructure, including supporting the expansion of transportation networks.

281.

He had a deep understanding of the law and legal principles, and his legal opinions and interpretations were highly regarded.

282.

Randolph was a strong supporter of American industry and advocated for protective tariffs to promote domestic manufacturing.

283.

He had a reputation for being reserved and somewhat aloof, but he was respected for his intellect and integrity.

284.

Randolph's contributions to the development of American government and law have had a lasting impact on the country's political structure.

285.

He was a prolific writer, penning numerous legal treatises and political essays throughout his career.

286.

Randolph was a mentor to many young lawyers and politicians, including future Chief Justice John Marshall.

287.

He played a key role in the creation of the Virginia Declaration of Rights, which served as a model for the Bill of Rights in the United States Constitution.

288.

Randolph was a strong advocate for a strong national defense and played a role in the establishment of the United States Navy.

289.

He was known for his meticulous attention to detail and thoroughness in legal and political matters.

290.

Randolph was a dedicated family man and had a close relationship with his wife, Elizabeth Nicholas Randolph, and their children.

291.

He was an avid reader and had a vast personal library that reflected his wide-ranging interests and intellectual curiosity.

292.

Randolph's legacy is honored through various institutions and landmarks named after him, including Randolph College in Virginia.

293.

He remained active in public life even after retiring from political office, continuing to contribute to legal and political discussions.

294.

Randolph was a proponent of a strong central government but also recognized the importance of protecting individual rights and liberties.

295.

He believed in the importance of education and was a supporter of public schools and universities.

296.

Randolph was known for his ability to navigate political alliances and build consensus among different factions.

297.

He played a key role in the creation of the federal court system, helping to shape the judiciary branch of government.

298.

Randolph's legal expertise and knowledge of constitutional law made him a trusted advisor to many political leaders of his time.

299.

He was a staunch advocate for the rights of states and believed in the principle of federalism as a way to maintain a balance of power.

300.

Randolph's contributions to the early American government helped establish the framework for a strong and enduring republic.

301.

George Read was born on September 18, 1733, in Cecil County, Maryland.

302.

He was a prominent American lawyer and politician during the Revolutionary era.

303.

Read graduated from the Philadelphia College (now the University of Pennsylvania) in 1753.

304.

He studied law in London and was admitted to the bar in 1753.

305.

Read settled in New Castle, Delaware, where he established a successful law practice.

306.

He served as the attorney general of Delaware from 1763 to 1774.

307.

Read was a delegate to the Stamp Act Congress in 1765, where he opposed British taxation policies.

308.

He played a leading role in the creation of the Delaware State Constitution in 1776, becoming the state's first Chief Justice.

309.

Read was a signer of the United States Declaration of Independence in 1776, representing Delaware.

310.

He served as a delegate to the Continental Congress from 1774 to 1777 and again from 1778 to 1782.

311.

Read was one of only two individuals to sign all three foundational documents of the United States: the Declaration of Independence, the Articles of Confederation, and the United States Constitution.

312.

He played a key role in the ratification of the United States Constitution, supporting its adoption at the Delaware Convention.

313.

Read served as a U.S. Senator from Delaware from 1789 to 1793.

314.

He was known for his strong support of the federal government and a centralized system of governance.

315.

Read was appointed as an Associate Justice of the Supreme Court of the United States by President George Washington in 1793, a position he held until his death.

316.

He was the only Supreme Court Justice to have previously signed the Declaration of Independence.

317.

Read's legal expertise and experience made him a respected and influential member of the Supreme Court.

318.

He was known for his strict interpretation of the Constitution and adherence to the principles of federalism.

319.

Read played a crucial role in several significant Supreme Court cases, including Ware v. Hylton, which dealt with the conflict between state and federal law.

320.

He retired from the Supreme Court in 1796 but continued to be active in public life and legal practice.

321.

Read was appointed as the Chancellor of Delaware in 1799, a position he held until his death.

322.

He was a strong advocate for religious freedom and played a key role in the passage of the Delaware Act of Toleration.

323.

Read was a member of the American Philosophical Society and corresponded with notable figures such as Benjamin Franklin and Thomas Jefferson.

324.

He was deeply committed to public service and held numerous positions in Delaware government, including serving as Speaker of the Delaware House of Assembly.

325.

Read was a supporter of the abolition of slavery and voted in favor of the Pennsylvania Gradual Abolition Act of 1780.

326.

He was a dedicated family man and had five children with his wife Gertrude Ross Till.

327.

Read's legal career spanned several decades, and he argued cases at all levels of the court system, including the United States Supreme Court.

328.

He was known for his intelligence, integrity, and eloquence, making him a respected figure in the legal and political spheres.

329.

Read's property, known as "Read House & Gardens," is now a historic site and museum in New Castle, Delaware.

330.

He was a proponent of strong state governments and worked to strike a balance between state and federal powers.

331.

Read's legal opinions and writings on constitutional law continue to be studied and referenced by legal scholars.

332.

He was involved in the early efforts to establish a national bank and played a role in the development of American financial institutions.

333.

Read was a supporter of a strong national defense and played a role in the organization of the Continental Army during the Revolutionary War.

334.

He had a reputation for being fair and impartial in his legal decisions and was known for his commitment to justice.

335.

Read's advocacy for strong federal power and a centralized government put him at odds with some anti-federalists in Delaware.

336.

He was an active participant in the political and social life of Delaware, attending social gatherings and engaging in public discourse.

337.

Read was a member of the committee that drafted the Articles of Confederation, the first constitution of the United States.

338.

He played a key role in resolving the boundary disputes between Delaware and neighboring states.

339.

Read's commitment to public service extended beyond his legal and political career. He was involved in charitable and educational endeavors in Delaware.

340.

He was a delegate to the Annapolis Convention in 1786, which laid the groundwork for the Constitutional Convention the following year.

341.

Read was a strong advocate for individual rights and liberties and was influential in shaping the Bill of Rights.

342.

He was a member of the Federalist Party and supported the policies of President George Washington.

343.

Read's contributions to the establishment of the United States as a sovereign nation are widely recognized and celebrated.

344.

He was a skilled orator and used his persuasive abilities to advocate for the principles of the American Revolution.

345.

Read was deeply committed to the principles of liberty, equality, and justice, which guided his actions and decisions throughout his life.

346.

He played a role in shaping the early legal system of Delaware, helping to establish the state's courts and legal procedures.

347.

Read's influence extended beyond Delaware, as he was well-respected and sought after for his legal expertise throughout the country.

348.

He was known for his strong work ethic and dedication to public service, often taking on multiple responsibilities simultaneously.

349.

Read's commitment to the ideals of the American Revolution and the principles of the Constitution earned him the admiration of his peers.

350.

He died on September 21, 1798, in New Castle, Delaware, leaving behind a legacy of service, leadership, and dedication to the principles of American democracy.

351.

The Black Mamba (Dendroaspis polylepis) is one of the most venomous snakes in the world.

352.

Despite its name, the Black Mamba is not entirely black. It typically has a sleek, olive to dark brown coloration.

353.

Black Mambas are found in parts of sub-Saharan Africa, primarily in savannah and rocky areas.

354.

They are known for their incredible speed and agility, capable of reaching speeds of up to 12 miles per hour (20 kilometers per hour).

355.

Black Mambas can grow to an average length of 8 to 10 feet (2.5 to 3 meters), with some individuals recorded to be over 14 feet (4.5 meters) long.

356.

These snakes have long, slender bodies and a coffin-shaped head.

357.

Black Mambas have extremely potent venom that is primarily neurotoxic, affecting the nervous system of their prey.

358.

Their venom can cause respiratory failure, paralysis, and even death if left untreated.

359.

Despite their deadly reputation, Black Mambas generally prefer to avoid confrontation and will retreat if given the opportunity.

360.

When threatened, they raise their heads, open their mouths, and display the black interior of their mouths as a warning sign.

361.

Black Mambas are diurnal, meaning they are most active during the day.

362.

They are highly skilled climbers and can scale trees with ease.

363.

Black Mambas have excellent eyesight and are capable of spotting prey from a considerable distance.

364.

Their diet primarily consists of small mammals, such as rodents, as well as birds and occasionally other reptiles.

365.

They have been observed hunting and consuming prey larger than themselves, including small antelope.

366.

Black Mambas possess a unique respiratory system that allows them to take in large amounts of oxygen, enhancing their endurance.

367.

They have been known to defend their territories aggressively against other snakes, including their own species.

368.

The average lifespan of a Black Mamba in the wild is estimated to be around 11 years.

369.

Females generally lay 10 to 25 eggs in underground nests and then leave them to incubate.

370.

The eggs hatch after approximately 2 to 3 months, and the young are fully independent from birth.

371.

Juvenile Black Mambas have a yellowish-brown coloration, which gradually darkens as they mature.

372.

The name "Black Mamba" is derived from the dark coloration inside their mouths, which is displayed as a warning sign when threatened.

373.

Black Mambas are often regarded as one of Africa's most iconic and feared snakes.

374.

They have been featured in various African cultures and folklore, symbolizing power, danger, and respect.

375.

Despite their venomous nature, Black Mambas also play a crucial ecological role as predators, helping to control rodent populations.

376.

The venom of a Black Mamba is not only potent but also fast-acting. Victims can experience symptoms within 15 minutes after a bite.

377.

Anti-venom is the primary treatment for Black Mamba envenomation, and prompt medical attention is crucial for survival.

378.

Black Mambas have been recorded to deliver multiple bites in rapid succession when provoked, increasing the amount of venom injected.

379.

Their strike distance can reach up to 40% of their body length, allowing them to strike from a significant distance.

380.

Black Mambas shed their skin regularly, approximately every 2 to 3 months, to accommodate their growth.

381.

They are solitary snakes and are not known to form social groups or exhibit communal behaviors.

382.

The nervous system effects of Black Mamba venom can lead to muscle paralysis and loss of coordination in prey.

383.

Black Mambas are highly sensitive to vibrations and can detect approaching threats through their specialized sensory organs.

384.

These snakes have a highly developed Jacobson's organ, which enables them to "taste" the air and detect chemical cues.

385.

They have a relatively small head compared to their body size, allowing for swift movement through tight spaces.

386.

Black Mambas have a reputation for being aggressive and defensive, but most bites occur when humans accidentally encounter them.

387.

These snakes have a keen sense of smell, which aids in locating prey and potential mates.

388.

Black Mambas have a high metabolic rate, which contributes to their energetic lifestyle and need for regular food intake.

389.

They are known for their distinctive defensive display, in which they raise the front portion of their body and flatten their necks.

390.

Black Mambas possess long fangs at the front of their mouths, which are used to inject venom into their prey.

391.

They are capable of striking with great accuracy, often targeting the head or neck region of their prey to ensure a swift kill.

392.

Black Mambas are considered to be more aggressive during the mating season when competition for mates is high.

393.

Their venom has been studied for its potential medical applications, particularly in the field of pain management.

394.

Black Mambas are sensitive to changes in temperature and may alter their behavior accordingly to regulate their body heat.

395.

They have a slender body shape that allows them to move through narrow crevices and burrows in search of prey.

396.

Black Mambas are excellent swimmers and can traverse bodies of water if necessary.

397.

They have a highly developed digestive system, allowing them to consume large prey items and efficiently extract nutrients.

398.

Black Mambas are known to be quite vocal, producing hissing sounds as a warning signal when threatened.

399.

These snakes have a lifespan in captivity that can exceed 20 years with proper care and maintenance.

400.

Black Mambas are a subject of fascination for herpetologists and snake enthusiasts due to their striking appearance, deadly venom, and remarkable behaviors.

401.

The Black-necked Stilt (Himantopus mexicanus) is a striking wading bird known for its long, slender legs and distinctive black and white plumage.

402.

They are found in wetland habitats across North and South America, including marshes, mudflats, and shallow lakes.

403.

Black-necked Stilts are known for their incredibly long legs, which can measure up to 12 inches (30 cm) in length.

404.

They have a distinctive black neck and head, white underparts, and a long, thin bill.

405.

The average length of an adult Black-necked Stilt is around 14 to 16 inches (36 to 41 cm), with a wingspan of approximately 24 inches (61 cm).

406.

They have a unique feeding behavior, using their long legs to wade in shallow water and probe the mud for small invertebrates, insects, and aquatic plants.

407.

Black-necked Stilts are highly agile and can walk or run on mud or vegetation without sinking.

408.

They have webbed toes, which aid in swimming and provide stability while foraging in water.

409.

These birds are excellent flyers and have a graceful flight pattern, with slow, deliberate wingbeats.

410.

Black-necked Stilts are known for their elaborate courtship displays, which involve various visual and vocal behaviors to attract mates.

411.

During courtship, they perform a "proud walk" display, in which they strut with their wings extended and call out to potential mates.

412.

They typically nest on the ground in shallow depressions or on floating vegetation, often in close proximity to water.

413.

Both male and female Black-necked Stilts take part in building the nest and incubating the eggs.

414.

The female lays a clutch of 3 to 5 eggs, which are incubated for approximately 22 to 24 days.

415.

The chicks are precocial, meaning they are able to leave the nest shortly after hatching and can swim and forage for food.

416.

Black-necked Stilts are highly territorial and will defend their nesting areas from other birds and potential threats.

417.

They are vocal birds and use various calls to communicate with each other, including high-pitched whistles and sharp alarm calls.

418.

These birds are known to form loose breeding colonies, where multiple pairs nest in close proximity to each other.

419.

The lifespan of a Black-necked Stilt in the wild is estimated to be around 5 to 10 years, but they can live longer in captivity.

420.

They are highly adaptable and can tolerate a wide range of water conditions, including both freshwater and saltwater habitats.

421.

Black-necked Stilts are known to migrate to warmer regions during the winter, seeking more favorable foraging and nesting conditions.

422.

They are excellent swimmers and are capable of navigating through water with ease.

423.

These birds have a keen sense of sight and can detect movement from a considerable distance, allowing them to spot potential prey.

424.

Black-necked Stilts have a specialized adaptation called "cephalic salt glands" that allows them to excrete excess salt from their bodies, enabling them to live in saline environments.

425.

Black-necked Stilts are capable of standing on one leg for extended periods, which helps them conserve body heat and maintain balance while resting.

426.

They have been observed engaging in communal nesting behavior, where multiple pairs of stilts share a single nest or nest in close proximity.

427.

Black-necked Stilts are known to engage in "wing-flagging" displays, where they extend their wings partially or fully and vibrate them rapidly to intimidate intruders or defend their territory.

428.

These birds have a high-pitched, piercing call that is often heard during their courtship displays.

429.

They have a monogamous mating system, with pairs usually remaining together for the breeding season.

430.

They are diurnal birds, primarily active during the day and resting or roosting at night.

431.

Black-necked Stilts have a wide range of predators, including larger birds, mammals, and reptiles.

432.

They have a streamlined body shape, which allows them to move swiftly through water and navigate dense vegetation.

433.

These birds are known for their territorial defense behaviors, including wing flapping, bill jabbing, and aggressive vocalizations.

434.

Black-necked Stilts have been observed engaging in "anting" behavior, where they rub ants or other insects on their feathers, possibly to help remove parasites or to spread chemical compounds that deter pests.

435.

They are adept at balancing on uneven surfaces, thanks to their long legs and agile movements.

436.

Black-necked Stilts have a distinctive feeding behavior known as "foot-trembling," where they rapidly tap their feet on the ground to stir up prey and detect vibrations in the mud.

437.

These birds have a highly developed sense of hearing, allowing them to locate and capture prey even in low-light conditions.

438.

Black-necked Stilts are known to perform distraction displays, where they feign injury or act as if they are injured to divert potential threats away from their nests or chicks.

439.

They have been observed engaging in communal roosting, with multiple individuals gathering in large groups to rest or sleep.

440.

Black-necked Stilts are capable of remarkable flight speeds, reaching up to 40 miles per hour (64 km/h) during migratory movements or when evading predators.

441.

These birds have a specialized adaptation in their bills, which allows them to filter and separate food items from water or mud.

442.

Black-necked Stilts are highly social birds and often gather in large flocks during the non-breeding season.

443.

They have been known to migrate over long distances, with some populations traveling thousands of miles between their breeding and wintering grounds.

444.

These birds have a strong instinct for protecting their young, often engaging in distraction displays or aggressive behaviors to deter potential threats.

445.

Black-necked Stilts have excellent color vision, which helps them identify prey and potential mates based on visual cues.

446.

They are capable of swallowing small prey items whole, thanks to their flexible necks and throats.

447.

These birds have a distinctive courtship dance, which involves elaborate movements, calls, and displays to attract a mate.

448.

Black-necked Stilts are known to engage in "allopreening," where they groom and clean each other's feathers as a form of social bonding.

449.

They have a wide distribution range, with different subspecies found in various parts of the Americas.

450.

Black-necked Stilts are a common sight in wetland ecosystems and are often celebrated for their elegant appearance and graceful movements.

451.

San Bernardino Ranch is located in southeastern Arizona, near the border with Mexico.

452.

It is one of the oldest continuously operated cattle ranches in the United States, established in 1884.

453.

The ranch spans over 90,000 acres of land, comprising a mix of grassland, desert, and riparian habitats.

454.

San Bernardino Ranch is known for its diverse wildlife, including species such as pronghorn antelope, javelina, mule deer, and a variety of bird species.

455.

The ranch has a rich cultural history, with evidence of human habitation dating back thousands of years, including Native American artifacts and rock art sites.

456.

It was originally established as a mining and ranching operation, with silver and lead being extracted from nearby mines.

457.

The ranch has a significant impact on local conservation efforts, working to protect and restore native habitats and species.

458.

It has been designated as an Important Bird Area (IBA) by the National Audubon Society, highlighting its importance for bird conservation.

459.

San Bernardino Ranch is also home to several rare and endangered species, including the Mexican gray wolf and the Chiricahua leopard frog.

460.

The ranch offers various recreational activities, such as birdwatching, hiking, and wildlife photography.

461.

It is managed by the nonprofit organization Borderlands Restoration Network, which focuses on ecological restoration and community engagement.

462.

San Bernardino Ranch is part of the larger "Sky Island" region, known for its unique biodiversity and varied ecosystems.

463.

The ranch's landscape is characterized by rugged mountains, canyons, and grassy plains.

464.

It provides important migration corridors for wildlife, allowing them to move between different habitats and find food and shelter.

465.

The ranch has a working cattle operation, with a herd of cattle that graze on the vast grasslands.

466.

San Bernardino Ranch hosts educational programs and workshops, teaching visitors about sustainable land management practices and the importance of conservation.

467.

The ranch is a prime location for stargazing due to its remote location and lack of light pollution.

468.

It is part of the Madrean Archipelago, a biodiversity hotspot that stretches across parts of the United States and Mexico.

469.

San Bernardino Ranch is recognized for its efforts in sustainable agriculture, implementing practices that promote soil health and water conservation.

470.

The ranch is involved in scientific research, collaborating with universities and organizations to study and monitor the region's wildlife and ecosystems.

471.

It offers opportunities for volunteers to participate in conservation projects and habitat restoration activities.

472.

San Bernardino Ranch has been the backdrop for various films, documentaries, and photography projects due to its scenic beauty and diverse wildlife.

473.

The ranch's location along the Mexican border has led to unique cross-cultural collaborations and initiatives to promote conservation and community engagement.

474.

It is an important stopover site for migratory birds, providing essential resources for resting and refueling during their long journeys.

475.

San Bernardino Ranch has a rich botanical diversity, with numerous plant species adapted to the arid conditions of the Sonoran Desert.

476.

The ranch's historic buildings and structures provide a glimpse into the region's past, reflecting the architectural styles of the late 19th and early 20th centuries.

477.

It is a haven for nature enthusiasts, offering opportunities for birdwatching, wildlife observation, and exploring the natural beauty of the surrounding landscape.

478.

The ranch's water sources, including natural springs and ponds, attract a wide variety of wildlife, making it an excellent location for wildlife photography.

479.

San Bernardino Ranch is actively involved in land restoration projects, including the removal of invasive species and the reintroduction of native plants.

480.

It has implemented sustainable ranching practices that prioritize land conservation and the well-being of the cattle.

481.

The ranch's proximity to the Mexican border has resulted in collaborative efforts with Mexican conservation organizations to protect shared ecosystems and wildlife.

482.

San Bernardino Ranch is committed to promoting community involvement and education, hosting workshops and events that raise awareness about conservation and sustainable land management.

483.

It has a network of trails and paths that allow visitors to explore the ranch's diverse landscapes, including canyons, grasslands, and riparian areas.

484.

The ranch's riparian habitats provide crucial resources for a variety of wildlife, including water, food, and shelter.

485.

San Bernardino Ranch is part of a larger conservation corridor that aims to connect and protect important habitats across the region.

486.

It has a resident biologist who conducts research and monitoring activities to assess the health of the ranch's ecosystems.

487.

The ranch collaborates with local schools and educational institutions, providing opportunities for students to learn about ecology, conservation, and sustainable agriculture.

488.

San Bernardino Ranch has a dedicated team of staff and volunteers who work tirelessly to maintain and protect the ranch's natural and cultural heritage.

489.

The ranch's scenic beauty and tranquility make it a popular destination for nature retreats and eco-tourism.

490.

It offers guided tours and interpretive programs, providing visitors with insights into the ranch's history, ecology, and conservation efforts.

491.

San Bernardino Ranch is located within the traditional territories of Indigenous communities, and efforts are made to respect and honor their cultural heritage.

492.

The ranch's open spaces and pristine landscapes provide opportunities for solitude and reflection, allowing visitors to reconnect with nature.

493.

It has a diverse array of reptiles and amphibians, including several species of snakes, lizards, and frogs.

494.

The ranch's wildlife monitoring programs help track population trends and inform conservation strategies for sensitive species.

495.

San Bernardino Ranch is a designated "dark sky" area, meaning that it has minimal artificial light pollution, allowing for exceptional stargazing experiences.

496.

It has a weather monitoring station that collects data on temperature, precipitation, and other climatic variables to better understand the ranch's ecosystems.

497.

The ranch's conservation initiatives include habitat restoration, erosion control, and the establishment of wildlife corridors.

498.

San Bernardino Ranch is located within the Chiricahua-Peloncillo Conservation Area, a region known for its high biodiversity and unique ecological features.

499.

It has a dedicated volunteer program that offers individuals the opportunity to contribute to conservation projects and learn about land stewardship.

500.

The ranch's conservation efforts extend beyond its boundaries, with collaborations and partnerships aimed at protecting and restoring ecosystems across the larger landscape.

501.

San Cayetano de Calabazas is an archaeological site located in southern Arizona, near the town of Tumacacori.

502.

The site is a historic Spanish mission that was established in the late 18th century.

503.

It was founded in 1756 by Jesuit missionaries as a mission to the indigenous O'odham people.

504.

San Cayetano de Calabazas was one of several missions in the region that aimed to convert Native Americans to Christianity and introduce European agricultural practices.

505.

The mission was named after Saint Cajetan of Thiene, the patron saint of job seekers and the unemployed.

506.

The site consists of the remains of a church, living quarters, workshops, and agricultural fields.

507.

The architecture of the mission reflects Spanish colonial influences, with adobe walls and traditional Spanish-style bell towers.

508.

San Cayetano de Calabazas was abandoned in the early 19th century due to various factors, including conflicts with local tribes and the secularization of Spanish missions.

509.

The mission site has been excavated by archaeologists, revealing artifacts and structures that provide insights into the daily life of the mission community.

510.

San Cayetano de Calabazas is listed on the National Register of Historic Places, recognizing its historical and cultural significance.

511.

The mission played a role in the Spanish colonization of the region, serving as a center for religious and cultural activities.

512.

The mission's location near the Santa Cruz River provided access to water for irrigation and agriculture.

513.

San Cayetano de Calabazas was part of a network of missions that extended across the Spanish colonial territories in the Americas.

514.

The mission site offers visitors an opportunity to learn about the region's colonial history and the interactions between European settlers and Native American communities.

515.

The site has interpretive signage and walking paths that guide visitors through the archaeological remains and provide historical context.

516.

San Cayetano de Calabazas is managed by the National Park Service as part of the Tumacácori National Historical Park.

517.

The mission site is located within the traditional lands of the O'odham people, and efforts are made to respect their cultural heritage and connections to the area.

518.

San Cayetano de Calabazas is an example of the cultural exchange and blending of traditions that occurred during the Spanish colonial period.

519.

The mission's agricultural practices introduced new crops and farming techniques to the region, contributing to the local economy and food production.

520.

San Cayetano de Calabazas is surrounded by the natural beauty of the Sonoran Desert, with its iconic saguaro cacti and diverse wildlife.

521.

The mission site provides a glimpse into the challenges and hardships faced by early European settlers and their efforts to establish a foothold in a new land.

522.

The ruins of the mission are a reminder of the complexities of colonial history, including the impacts on indigenous communities and the cultural transformations that occurred.

523.

San Cayetano de Calabazas is an important archaeological site, offering valuable information about the material culture and architecture of Spanish missions in the Southwest.

524.

The mission's location near other historic sites, such as the nearby Tumacácori Mission, allows visitors to explore multiple facets of the region's history.

525.

San Cayetano de Calabazas is situated in a scenic area, surrounded by rolling hills and picturesque landscapes.

526.

The mission site has been the subject of ongoing research and study, with archaeologists uncovering new information about its history and significance.

527.

The mission's construction and layout reflect the Spanish colonial approach to town planning, with a central plaza and buildings arranged in a specific pattern.

528.

San Cayetano de Calabazas played a role in the larger network of Spanish missions that extended from Mexico into present-day Arizona and California.

529.

The mission's decline and abandonment were influenced by various factors, including disease, conflicts with indigenous groups, and changing political dynamics.

530.

San Cayetano de Calabazas offers a glimpse into the daily life of the mission community, including their religious practices, agricultural activities, and interactions with neighboring settlements.

531.

The mission site has been the focus of conservation efforts to preserve and protect the remaining structures and artifacts.

532.

San Cayetano de Calabazas is a place of historical significance and serves as a reminder of the complex and interconnected histories of the Southwest.

533.

The mission's location near the international border between the United States and Mexico highlights the transnational nature of its history and cultural influences.

534.

San Cayetano de Calabazas is a popular destination for history enthusiasts, archaeologists, and those interested in the region's colonial past.

535.

The mission site has been used as a backdrop for cultural events, reenactments, and educational programs that bring its history to life.

536.

San Cayetano de Calabazas provides opportunities for visitors to engage with the site through guided tours, self-guided exploration, and interpretive programs.

537.

The mission's ruins are a testament to the passage of time and the resilience of the structures that were once integral to the mission community.

538.

San Cayetano de Calabazas is located in a region known for its rich cultural heritage, with other archaeological sites and historical landmarks nearby.

539.

The mission's architectural features, such as its arched doorways and bell towers, showcase the craftsmanship and design skills of the period.

540.

San Cayetano de Calabazas has inspired artistic representations, including paintings, photographs, and literature, capturing its historical and aesthetic significance.

541.

The mission's walls and foundations provide insights into the construction techniques used during the colonial period, including the use of adobe and locally sourced materials.

542.

San Cayetano de Calabazas offers visitors the opportunity to reflect on the complexities of colonialism, cultural exchange, and the legacies of European settlement in the Americas.

543.

The mission's location near the Santa Cruz River allowed for transportation and trade, connecting the mission community to regional networks.

544.

San Cayetano de Calabazas has been the subject of archaeological investigations since the early 20th century, contributing to our understanding of the mission era.

545.

The mission site is surrounded by natural habitats that support a variety of wildlife, making it a potential destination for nature enthusiasts and birdwatchers.

546.

San Cayetano de Calabazas is an important cultural site for both local communities and visitors from around the world, showcasing the region's diverse heritage.

547.

The mission's architecture and layout reflect the blending of European and indigenous influences, creating a distinct visual and cultural identity.

548.

San Cayetano de Calabazas provides opportunities for interdisciplinary research, combining archaeological, historical, and cultural perspectives.

549.

The mission's historical significance extends beyond its founding and abandonment, encompassing the broader narratives of colonization, religion, and cultural exchange.

550.

San Cayetano de Calabazas serves as a reminder of the long-standing human presence in the region and the ongoing efforts to preserve and interpret its history.

551.

William Rittenhouse was a German-born American Mennonite, born in 1644 in the Duchy of Pfalz, Germany.

552.

He is known as the founder of the first paper mill in British North America.

553.

Rittenhouse immigrated to America in 1688, settling in Germantown, Pennsylvania.

554.

In 1690, he established the first paper mill in British North America on the banks of the Wissahickon Creek in Germantown.

555.

The mill was operated by the Rittenhouse family for several generations, becoming a successful and prominent business.

556.

Rittenhouse was known for his exceptional craftsmanship and technical skills, which contributed to the success of his paper mill.

557.

He used a water-powered wheel to grind rags into pulp, which was
then formed into sheets of paper.

558.

The paper produced at Rittenhouse's mill was of high quality and
was in great demand for various purposes, including printing
newspapers, books, and legal documents.

559.

Rittenhouse's paper mill played a significant role in promoting
literacy and education in the early colonies, as it provided a local
source of paper for printing materials.

560.

He also pioneered the use of watermarking in paper production,
which added a unique identifier to each sheet of paper, making it
difficult to forge or counterfeit.

561.

Rittenhouse's paper mill was a vital part of the economic
development of Germantown, contributing to the growth of the
community.

562.

He trained his sons, Nicholas and William Jr., in the papermaking
trade, ensuring the continuity of the family business.

563.

Rittenhouse was an active member of the Mennonite community and
contributed to the establishment of the first Mennonite meetinghouse
in Germantown.

564.

He was involved in local governance and served as a justice of the
peace in Germantown.

565.

Rittenhouse's descendants made significant contributions to various fields, including science, engineering, and politics.

566.

His grandson, David Rittenhouse, became a renowned astronomer, mathematician, and inventor, serving as the first director of the United States Mint.

567.

William Rittenhouse's paper mill remained in operation for more than a century, continuing to produce paper until it was demolished in the early 19th century.

568.

Today, the Rittenhouse Paper Mill is commemorated as a historical landmark, representing an important chapter in the history of American papermaking.

569.

Rittenhouse's entrepreneurial spirit and innovation contributed to the growth of the paper industry in America.

570.

His paper mill laid the foundation for the development of a thriving printing and publishing industry in the colonies.

571.

Rittenhouse's work helped reduce dependence on imported paper, fostering self-sufficiency in the early American colonies.

572.

The success of his paper mill inspired others to establish similar mills across the country, further advancing the papermaking industry.

573.

Rittenhouse's dedication to quality and craftsmanship set a high standard for paper production in America.

574.

His business acumen and entrepreneurial skills made him a respected figure in the community.

575.

Rittenhouse's paper mill created employment opportunities for the local population, contributing to the economic prosperity of Germantown.

576.

The paper produced at Rittenhouse's mill was known for its strength and durability, making it highly sought after by printers and publishers.

577.

Rittenhouse's entrepreneurial venture helped foster cultural and intellectual growth in the colonies by providing access to affordable paper for books and publications.

578.

His paper mill played a role in the dissemination of knowledge and ideas, supporting the development of a literate society.

579.

Rittenhouse's work showcased the importance of skilled craftsmanship and technical expertise in the early American economy.

580.

He made significant contributions to the development of the papermaking industry, which had a profound impact on the growth of printing and publishing in America.

581.

Rittenhouse's paper mill helped establish Germantown as a center for printing and paper production in the colonies.

582.

His entrepreneurial success inspired other immigrants and settlers to pursue their own ventures, contributing to the overall economic growth of the colonies.

583.

Rittenhouse's paper mill utilized advanced techniques and machinery for the time, showcasing his commitment to innovation.

584.

He fostered a sense of community by providing a reliable source of paper and supporting local printers and publishers.

585.

Rittenhouse's business legacy influenced future generations of papermakers, contributing to the continued growth and development of the industry.

586.

His work played a role in shaping the cultural and intellectual landscape of the American colonies, paving the way for the spread of knowledge and ideas.

587.

Rittenhouse's paper mill exemplified the spirit of entrepreneurship and resourcefulness that defined early colonial America.

588.

His success in the papermaking industry contributed to the economic stability of Germantown, attracting further investment and development.

589.

Rittenhouse's commitment to craftsmanship and quality helped establish American-made paper as a respected and valued product.

590.

His entrepreneurial endeavors demonstrate the importance of individual initiative and innovation in driving economic progress.

591.

Rittenhouse's paper mill served as a hub of activity, bringing together workers, craftsmen, and merchants in the local community.

592.

He faced various challenges in establishing and operating his paper mill, including sourcing raw materials, maintaining equipment, and managing a skilled workforce.

593.

Rittenhouse's entrepreneurial journey reflects the perseverance and determination of early settlers in building a prosperous future.

594.

His paper mill played a role in preserving and disseminating important historical and cultural documents of the time.

595.

Rittenhouse's success in the papermaking industry helped establish a sense of pride and self-sufficiency among the colonists.

596.

His innovative approach to paper production contributed to the growth of printing as a profession, creating employment opportunities for skilled workers.

597.

Rittenhouse's paper mill was not only a center of industry but also a gathering place for intellectual and cultural exchange.

598.

He actively sought to improve the efficiency and quality of paper production, experimenting with new techniques and materials.

599.

Rittenhouse's entrepreneurial spirit and dedication to his craft left a lasting impact on the papermaking industry in America.

600.

His contributions to the development of papermaking techniques and practices helped shape the industry's future growth and success.

601.

The Black-necked Stilt (Himantopus mexicanus) is a striking wading bird known for its long, thin legs and black-and-white plumage.

602.

It is found in wetland habitats across the Americas, including North America, Central America, and parts of South America.

603.

The Black-necked Stilt is highly adapted for wading in shallow water, with its long legs allowing it to navigate through marshes, ponds, and mudflats.

604.

Adult Black-necked Stilts typically measure around 14-16 inches (36-41 cm) in length, with a wingspan of approximately 24-27 inches (61-69 cm).

605.

The males and females of this species are similar in appearance, with both exhibiting black and white plumage and long, thin bills.

606.

The name "Black-necked Stilt" refers to the bird's black neck and head, contrasting with its white belly and underparts.

607.

These stilts have distinctive pink legs, which provide a striking contrast to their black and white feathers.

608.

They have a graceful and elegant appearance, often seen wading slowly in shallow water as they search for food.

609.

Black-necked Stilts are known for their distinctive vocalizations, including high-pitched yelps and sharp alarm calls.

610.

They are primarily carnivorous and feed on a diet consisting of small invertebrates such as insects, crustaceans, and mollusks.

611.

The long, slender bill of the Black-necked Stilt is perfectly adapted for capturing and probing into the water to catch prey.

612.

During breeding season, male Black-necked Stilts engage in courtship displays to attract females. These displays involve various movements, wing flapping, and vocalizations.

613.

Nests are built on the ground, often in shallow water or on floating vegetation. The nests are shallow depressions lined with twigs, grass, and other vegetation.

614.

Female Black-necked Stilts typically lay a clutch of three to five eggs, which are incubated by both parents for about three weeks.

615.

Once hatched, the chicks are precocial, meaning they are relatively independent and able to walk and swim shortly after hatching.

616.

Black-necked Stilts are highly protective parents and will aggressively defend their nesting territory and offspring.

617.

These birds are known for their elaborate and intricate mating dances, involving coordinated movements and vocalizations.

618.

They are social birds and often gather in large flocks, especially during migration and wintering periods.

619.

The Black-necked Stilt has an excellent sense of sight, allowing it to detect prey and potential threats from a distance.

620.

They are well adapted for wading in water, with specialized adaptations such as webbed feet and long toes that distribute their weight and prevent sinking into soft substrates.

621.

The Black-necked Stilt is considered a flagship species for wetland conservation, as its presence indicates a healthy and diverse ecosystem.

622.

Despite their elegant appearance, Black-necked Stilts are fierce defenders of their territories and will aggressively chase away intruders.

623.

They have a wide distribution and can be found in a variety of wetland habitats, including marshes, ponds, lagoons, and estuaries.

624.

Black-necked Stilts are excellent swimmers and can navigate through water with ease using their long legs and webbed feet.

625.

These birds have a lifespan of around 5-10 years in the wild, although some individuals have been known to live longer.

626.

Black-necked Stilts are highly adaptable and can tolerate a wide range of water salinity levels, allowing them to occupy both freshwater and brackish habitats.

627.

They are known to engage in "foot-trembling" behavior, where they rapidly vibrate their legs to stir up prey in the water.

628.

Black-necked Stilts are monogamous and form long-term pair bonds with their mates, often returning to the same breeding site year after year.

629.

In some regions, these birds are migratory, undertaking seasonal movements to seek more favorable feeding and breeding grounds.

630.

They are agile fliers and can fly with their long legs extended behind them, creating an elegant and distinctive silhouette in flight.

631.

Black-necked Stilts have excellent coordination and balance, which allows them to navigate across unstable substrates such as mud and vegetation.

632.

The population of Black-necked Stilts is generally stable, although habitat loss and degradation remain significant threats to their long-term survival.

633.

They are highly vocal birds and use various calls to communicate with other members of their flock and defend their territory.

634.

Black-necked Stilts have a diverse range of behaviors, including preening, bathing, foraging, and engaging in social interactions.

635.

These birds have an interesting reproductive strategy known as "egg-dumping," where they lay their eggs in the nests of other stilts, often within the same breeding colony.

636.

Black-necked Stilts are known to engage in communal nesting, where multiple pairs nest close to each other, providing additional protection against predators.

637.

They are efficient hunters and can quickly snatch small prey items such as insects and small fish from the water's surface.

638.

Black-necked Stilts have excellent eyesight both above and below the water, allowing them to locate and capture prey accurately.

639.

They are agile and quick in their movements, enabling them to swiftly respond to changes in their environment and avoid potential threats.

640.

Black-necked Stilts are highly adaptable to human-altered environments and can be found in agricultural areas, salt pans, and even urban wetlands.

641.

They are known to engage in "broken-wing" displays as a distraction technique to lure predators away from their nesting sites.

642.

Black-necked Stilts are diurnal birds, meaning they are most active during daylight hours and rest or sleep during the night.

643.

These birds have a hierarchical social structure within their flocks, with dominant individuals having priority access to resources and breeding opportunities.

644.

Black-necked Stilts have excellent heat tolerance and can withstand extreme temperatures, thanks to their ability to regulate their body temperature through behavioral adaptations such as shading and evaporative cooling.

645.

They are known to engage in "allopreening," a behavior in which they groom and clean the feathers of other members of their flock, promoting social bonding and maintaining feather health.

646.

Black-necked Stilts have a diverse range of vocalizations, including contact calls, alarm calls, and courtship calls, each serving a specific communication purpose.

647.

These birds have a high metabolic rate and require a substantial amount of food to fuel their energy needs, especially during the breeding season.

648.

Black-necked Stilts have long, flexible necks, which they use to reach into the water and capture prey without fully submerging their bodies.

649.

They have a wide distribution and can be found in a variety of wetland habitats, including salt marshes, brackish estuaries, and coastal lagoons.

650.

Black-necked Stilts are fascinating birds that exhibit a range of behaviors, adaptations, and social dynamics, making them a subject of interest for birdwatchers, ecologists, and nature enthusiasts.

651.

The Black Rhinoceros (Diceros bicornis) is a large, herbivorous mammal native to Africa.

652.

It is one of the two species of rhinoceros found in Africa, with the other being the White Rhinoceros.

653.

Despite its name, the Black Rhinoceros is not entirely black but rather has a grayish-brown to black coloration, which helps it blend into its environment.

654.

They are known for their prehensile upper lip, which they use to grasp and pull vegetation while feeding.

655.

Black Rhinos have two large horns made of keratin, a protein found in hair and nails. The front horn is usually longer and can reach lengths of up to 1.5 meters (5 feet).

656.

These rhinos have a thick, armored skin that protects them from thorny vegetation and potential predators.

657.

Adult Black Rhinoceroses can weigh between 800 and 1,400 kilograms (1,800 to 3,100 pounds), with males being slightly larger than females.

658.

They have a distinctive hump on their neck, which is formed by a large muscle mass that supports their massive head.

659.

Black Rhinos have a relatively short, stout body with stocky legs, allowing them to move quickly and navigate through dense vegetation.

660.

These rhinos are solitary animals and are known for their territorial behavior, marking their territories with urine and dung piles.

661.

They have poor eyesight but compensate with excellent hearing and a keen sense of smell, which helps them detect predators and locate food.

662.

Black Rhinoceroses are browsers, feeding mainly on leaves, twigs, and branches from a variety of plants.

663.

Despite their size, they are agile and can reach speeds of up to 55 kilometers per hour (34 mph) when threatened.

664.

The Black Rhino is critically endangered, with population numbers declining rapidly due to poaching and habitat loss.

665.

Historically, they were found across much of sub-Saharan Africa, but their range has significantly decreased, and they are now confined to a few select regions.

666.

Black Rhinos are categorized into four subspecies: Western Black Rhino, Eastern Black Rhino, Southern Central Black Rhino, and Southwestern Black Rhino.

667.

The Eastern Black Rhino is the most numerous and widespread of the subspecies, while the Western Black Rhino is considered extinct.

668.

They have a complex social structure, and while they are generally solitary, they may come together in loose groups during feeding or watering.

669.

Black Rhinos communicate through a variety of vocalizations, including snorts, grunts, and bellows, which are used for establishing dominance or attracting mates.

670.

The gestation period for a Black Rhino is approximately 15 to 16 months, one of the longest gestation periods among land mammals.

671.

A female Black Rhino typically gives birth to a single calf, which stays with her for about two to three years before becoming independent.

672.

Calves have a reddish-brown coloration, which gradually darkens as they mature.

673.

Black Rhinos have an average lifespan of 30 to 40 years in the wild, although some individuals have been known to live up to 50 years.

674.

These rhinos have a specialized lip structure that allows them to selectively browse and feed on specific plant species.

675.

Black Rhinos play a crucial role in their ecosystem by shaping the vegetation through their feeding behavior, creating openings for other animals to access food.

676.

They are known to use mud wallows to cool down and protect their skin from insects and the sun's harmful rays.

677.

Despite their large size, Black Rhinos are excellent swimmers and can traverse rivers and water bodies with ease.

678.

The horns of Black Rhinoceroses are highly sought after in the illegal wildlife trade, primarily for their use in traditional medicine and as status symbols.

679.

Conservation efforts, such as anti-poaching initiatives and habitat protection, are crucial for the survival of Black Rhinos in the wild.

680.

Rhino horn trade is internationally banned, but illegal poaching remains a significant threat to their survival.

681.

Black Rhinoceroses have been successfully reintroduced into some protected areas, contributing to their conservation and population recovery.

682.

Their conservation status is closely monitored by various organizations, including the International Union for Conservation of Nature (IUCN).

683.

In some cultures, the Black Rhino is considered a symbol of power and strength and is featured in traditional folklore and artwork.

684.

Black Rhinos have thick, padded feet with three toes, which help distribute their weight and allow them to move quietly and efficiently.

685.

They are primarily active during the cooler hours of the day, often resting in shaded areas during the hottest part of the day.

686.

Black Rhinos have a unique and complex digestive system that allows them to extract maximum nutrients from the plant material they consume.

687.

These rhinos have been observed engaging in a behavior known as "wallowing," where they roll in mud or water to cool down and remove parasites from their skin.

688.

Black Rhinos have few natural predators in the wild, but they may occasionally fall victim to lions or hyenas, particularly vulnerable calves.

689.

The skin of Black Rhinoceroses is highly sensitive and prone to sunburn, which is why they often seek shade during the hottest hours.

690.

Black Rhinos have a keen sense of hearing and can detect sounds over long distances, helping them avoid potential threats.

691.

They have a strong jaw and powerful bite, allowing them to break through tough vegetation and browse on branches and twigs.

692.

Black Rhinoceroses have well-developed muscles in their neck and shoulder region, giving them the strength and agility needed for their browsing behavior.

693.

They are known to be selective feeders, choosing specific parts of plants that are highly nutritious and avoiding those with low nutritional value.

694.

Black Rhinos have a complex vocal repertoire, including grunts, roars, and snorts, which they use for communication and to establish dominance.

695.

The horns of Black Rhinoceroses are not attached to their skull but are composed of compressed hair-like fibers.

696.

Despite their size, Black Rhinos are surprisingly agile climbers and can navigate steep slopes and rocky terrain with ease.

697.

They have a well-developed sense of smell, which allows them to detect food sources and communicate with other rhinos through scent markings.

698.

Black Rhinoceroses are known to be relatively aggressive, especially when they feel threatened or during territorial disputes.

699.

Their horns continue to grow throughout their lifetime, and the length and shape of the horns can vary between individuals.

700.

Black Rhinos have a fascinating evolutionary history, with fossil evidence suggesting they have been around for millions of years, adapting to various ecological changes over time.

701.

San Xavier del Bac Mission, also known as the White Dove of the Desert, is a historic Spanish Catholic mission located in southern Arizona, USA.

702.

It was founded in 1692 by Father Eusebio Kino, a Jesuit missionary, and has been in continuous operation since its establishment.

703.

The mission is dedicated to Saint Francis Xavier, a prominent Catholic missionary and co-founder of the Jesuit Order.

704.

San Xavier del Bac Mission is considered one of the finest examples of Spanish Colonial architecture in the United States.

705.

The exterior of the mission features beautiful baroque and Moorish-inspired designs, with intricate carvings and decorative elements.

706.

The interior of the mission is adorned with elaborate frescoes, paintings, and sculptures, showcasing a blend of Spanish, Native American, and Mexican influences.

707.

San Xavier del Bac Mission is renowned for its ornate altar screen, known as a retablo, which is covered in gold leaf and features intricate religious artwork.

708.

The mission is still an active place of worship and serves as a parish church for the Tohono O'odham Nation, as well as the surrounding community.

709.

It is a significant pilgrimage site for both Catholic and non-Catholic visitors, attracting thousands of tourists each year.

710.

San Xavier del Bac Mission is located on the ancestral lands of the Tohono O'odham people, who have a strong historical and cultural connection to the site.

711.

The mission played a crucial role in the conversion of the local Native American population to Catholicism during the Spanish colonial period.

712.

The construction of the mission took several decades, with different phases of expansion and renovation occurring over the years.

713.

The mission's distinctive white facade is due to the use of a traditional lime-based plaster, which was applied to protect the adobe walls from weathering.

714.

San Xavier del Bac Mission has survived numerous challenges, including fires, earthquakes, and wars, thanks to ongoing restoration and preservation efforts.

715.

The mission's architecture and artwork reflect a fusion of Spanish and indigenous cultures, showcasing the historical and cultural exchange that took place during colonization.

716.

The mission is surrounded by a peaceful courtyard and garden, providing a serene environment for reflection and contemplation.

717.

San Xavier del Bac Mission is listed on the National Register of Historic Places and has been designated a National Historic Landmark.

718.

The mission attracts visitors not only for its religious significance but also for its historical, architectural, and artistic value.

719.

The bell tower of San Xavier del Bac Mission stands at 82 feet tall and is an iconic symbol of the mission.

720.

The mission is located near the Santa Cruz River, which played a vital role in the establishment and sustenance of the mission community.

721.

San Xavier del Bac Mission is known for its annual feast day celebration, held on December 9th, attracting thousands of pilgrims and participants.

722.

The mission's interior is filled with stunning murals depicting religious scenes and saints, created by Native American and Mexican artists.

723.

The mission's architecture incorporates both European and Native American building techniques, such as the use of adobe bricks and traditional O'odham construction methods.

724.

San Xavier del Bac Mission was largely self-sufficient, with its own orchards, gardens, and livestock providing sustenance for the community.

725.

The mission's location in the Sonoran Desert adds to its unique charm, with cacti and desert vegetation surrounding the area.

726.

San Xavier del Bac Mission has undergone extensive restoration and conservation efforts to preserve its historical and cultural significance.

727.

The mission has a small museum that showcases artifacts, religious objects, and historical information about the site and its significance.

728.

The mission's architecture and artwork reflect the multicultural influences of the region, serving as a testament to the blending of different traditions and aesthetics.

729.

San Xavier del Bac Mission has been featured in various films, documentaries, and literature, contributing to its recognition as a cultural and historical landmark.

730.

The mission's bell tower houses several bells of different sizes, each with its own unique sound and purpose.

731.

San Xavier del Bac Mission has served as a beacon of hope and spiritual guidance for generations of believers and continues to be an important religious site today.

732.

The mission's annual pilgrimage attracts people from diverse backgrounds, fostering a sense of community and shared devotion.

733.

San Xavier del Bac Mission has inspired numerous artists, writers, and photographers who have captured its beauty and significance through their work.

734.

The mission's richly decorated altar and sanctuary create a visually stunning and awe-inspiring atmosphere for worship.

735.

San Xavier del Bac Mission is known for its distinctive tower and dome, which can be seen from miles away, standing as a landmark in the surrounding landscape.

736.

The mission's archives hold a wealth of historical documents, including records of baptisms, marriages, and other significant events from the past centuries.

737.

San Xavier del Bac Mission has served as a place of refuge and spiritual solace for the Tohono O'odham people, providing a connection to their cultural heritage.

738.

The mission's patron saint, Saint Francis Xavier, is believed to be the guardian of travelers, making the site an important stop for those seeking safe journeys.

739.

San Xavier del Bac Mission has been recognized for its architectural significance and has received prestigious awards for its preservation and restoration efforts.

740.

The mission's annual Easter Vigil is a vibrant celebration of faith, featuring traditional music, dances, and religious rituals.

741.

San Xavier del Bac Mission has witnessed the passage of time and stands as a testament to the endurance of faith and cultural traditions.

742.

The mission's historic cemetery is the final resting place of many prominent individuals from the local community and mission history.

743.

San Xavier del Bac Mission offers guided tours for visitors, providing insights into its history, architecture, and religious significance.

744.

The mission's courtyard is often filled with colorful flowers, creating a picturesque setting for weddings, festivals, and other special events.

745.

San Xavier del Bac Mission is known for its welcoming and inclusive atmosphere, inviting people of all backgrounds to experience its beauty and spirituality.

746.

The mission's ceiling features intricate and colorful patterns, resembling traditional Native American designs, adding to its visual appeal.

747.

San Xavier del Bac Mission serves as a hub for cultural exchange, hosting events that celebrate both Native American and Hispanic traditions.

748.

The mission's chapel is a sacred space where visitors can light candles, offer prayers, and experience a sense of tranquility and reverence.

749.

San Xavier del Bac Mission has been an important center for education, providing religious instruction and schooling for the local community.

750.

The mission's restoration projects have involved collaboration between experts from various fields, ensuring the preservation of its architectural and artistic heritage.

751.

Sierra Bonita Ranch is a historic cattle ranch located in southeastern Arizona, USA.

752.

The ranch was established in 1872 by Henry Hooker, a prominent cattleman and entrepreneur.

753.

It covers an area of over 100,000 acres and includes diverse landscapes such as grasslands, forests, and canyons.

754.

Sierra Bonita Ranch has been in continuous operation for over 150 years, making it one of the oldest working ranches in Arizona.

755.

The ranch played a significant role in the development of the cattle industry in the region and the expansion of ranching operations in the American West.

756.

Sierra Bonita Ranch has a rich history of famous visitors, including notable figures such as Wyatt Earp and Doc Holliday, who were friends of Henry Hooker.

757.

The ranch is known for its picturesque scenery, with rolling hills, rugged mountains, and scenic vistas that attract nature lovers and outdoor enthusiasts.

758.

Sierra Bonita Ranch has diverse wildlife, including various bird species, mammals, and reptiles, making it a popular destination for wildlife observation and photography.

759.

The ranch is home to a working cattle operation, with herds of cattle grazing on its vast grasslands.

760.

Sierra Bonita Ranch has preserved its historic buildings, including the main ranch house, bunkhouses, barns, and corrals, which provide a glimpse into the ranch's past.

761.

The ranch house at Sierra Bonita is a two-story adobe structure that showcases the architectural style of the time and provides a glimpse into the life of early ranchers.

762.

Sierra Bonita Ranch has been featured in books, documentaries, and films, contributing to its recognition as a historic and cultural landmark.

763.

The ranch offers guided tours, allowing visitors to learn about its history, cattle operations, and the challenges and rewards of ranching in the region.

764.

Sierra Bonita Ranch hosts various events throughout the year, including cattle roundups, branding ceremonies, and cowboy festivals, offering visitors a chance to experience the cowboy way of life.

765.

The ranch's location near the Mexican border adds to its unique character, with influences from Mexican culture and traditions evident in the ranch's heritage.

766.

Sierra Bonita Ranch has been a family-owned and operated business for several generations, with the Hooker family maintaining its commitment to preserving the ranch's legacy.

767.

The ranch is a working example of sustainable land and resource management practices, with an emphasis on conservation and preserving the natural environment.

768.

Sierra Bonita Ranch has served as a place of inspiration for artists, writers, and photographers who have captured its beauty and the spirit of the American West.

769.

The ranch's proximity to national parks and recreational areas, such as the Chiricahua National Monument and Coronado National Forest, offers additional opportunities for outdoor exploration and adventure.

770.

Sierra Bonita Ranch is located in a region known for its rich Native American history, with archaeological sites and petroglyphs nearby, providing insights into the area's ancient civilizations.

771.

The ranch's vast acreage allows for various recreational activities, including hiking, horseback riding, fishing, and camping.

772.

Sierra Bonita Ranch has a diverse ecosystem, with plant species adapted to the arid climate, including cacti, desert shrubs, and grasses.

773.

The ranch's water sources, including natural springs and streams, provide crucial resources for both wildlife and livestock.

774.

Sierra Bonita Ranch has been involved in conservation efforts, partnering with organizations dedicated to preserving the region's natural resources and wildlife habitats.

775.

The ranch's historical significance and cultural heritage have led to its inclusion on the National Register of Historic Places.

776.

Sierra Bonita Ranch offers educational programs for students and visitors, providing opportunities to learn about ranching practices, local history, and the importance of land stewardship.

777.

The ranch's wide-open spaces and unspoiled landscapes offer a sense of tranquility and escape from the busy modern world.

778.

Sierra Bonita Ranch has a strong sense of community, with neighboring ranchers and local residents forming a tight-knit network that supports one another.

779.

The ranch's horseback riding trails allow visitors to explore the vast expanse of the property and experience the freedom of riding through open fields and wooded areas.

780.

Sierra Bonita Ranch has a rich cowboy and ranching heritage, with stories of cattle drives, rodeos, and cowboy legends passed down through generations.

781.

The ranch's dedication to sustainable agriculture practices includes rotational grazing and land restoration techniques to ensure the long-term health of the land.

782.

Sierra Bonita Ranch has a peaceful and serene atmosphere, offering visitors a chance to disconnect from the modern world and reconnect with nature.

783.

The ranch's sunsets are known for their breathtaking beauty, with vibrant colors painting the sky as the day comes to a close.

784.

Sierra Bonita Ranch is located in an area known for its dark skies, making it an ideal destination for stargazing and astronomy enthusiasts.

785.

The ranch's wildlife management programs aim to protect and enhance biodiversity, including the conservation of endangered species such as the Chiricahua leopard frog and Mexican gray wolf.

786.

Sierra Bonita Ranch is an important contributor to the local economy, providing employment opportunities and supporting local businesses and services.

787.

The ranch's commitment to preserving open spaces and maintaining the rural character of the region helps protect wildlife corridors and maintain the natural beauty of the area.

788.

Sierra Bonita Ranch has played a role in historical events and conflicts, including serving as a stopping point for cavalry troops during the Apache Wars.

789.

The ranch's water sources have historical and cultural significance, with tales of early settlers and Native American tribes relying on these vital resources.

790.

Sierra Bonita Ranch offers a glimpse into the daily life of a working ranch, showcasing the hard work, dedication, and resilience required to sustain a successful operation.

791.

The ranch's bird-watching opportunities attract bird enthusiasts from around the world, with species such as roadrunners, hummingbirds, and raptors frequenting the area.

792.

Sierra Bonita Ranch has a rich oral history, with stories of cattle rustlers, outlaws, and encounters with wildlife passed down through generations of ranchers.

793.

The ranch's proximity to the border region adds a unique cultural dynamic, with influences from both Mexican and American traditions evident in the local community.

794.

Sierra Bonita Ranch has been a backdrop for family gatherings, weddings, and special celebrations, creating lasting memories for generations.

795.

The ranch's scenic drives offer panoramic views of the surrounding mountains, valleys, and canyons, providing a memorable and immersive experience.

796.

Sierra Bonita Ranch has witnessed the changing landscapes of the American West, adapting to economic, environmental, and social challenges over the years.

797.

The ranch's working cowboys and ranch hands exemplify the spirit of the American cowboy, showcasing their horsemanship skills and dedication to their craft.

798.

Sierra Bonita Ranch's historic buildings and artifacts provide a glimpse into the past, showcasing the craftsmanship and ingenuity of early settlers and ranchers.

799.

The ranch's proximity to national forests and wilderness areas offers opportunities for outdoor recreation, including hunting, fishing, and wildlife observation.

800.

Sierra Bonita Ranch is a testament to the enduring spirit of the American West, representing a connection to the land, history, and cultural heritage of the region.

801.

Caesar Rodney was an American lawyer and politician who played a significant role in the American Revolution and the early years of the United States.

802.

He was born on October 7, 1728, in Dover, Delaware, and was raised on a tobacco plantation.

803.

Rodney received a classical education and studied law, eventually becoming one of Delaware's most prominent attorneys.

804.

He served as a militia officer during the French and Indian War, gaining military experience that would prove valuable in later years.

805.

Rodney entered politics and held various positions, including serving in the Delaware House of Assembly and as a delegate to the Continental Congress.

806.

In 1776, Rodney cast a crucial vote in favor of the Declaration of Independence while suffering from severe facial cancer. He famously rode overnight from Delaware to Philadelphia to break a tie vote.

807.

Despite his physical challenges, Rodney was known for his determination and resilience, earning him the nickname "The Noblest Roman of Them All."

808.

Rodney also played a vital role in Delaware's state government, serving as Speaker of the House, President of Delaware, and Chief Justice of the Delaware Supreme Court.

809.

He advocated for the abolition of slavery in Delaware and worked to reform the state's legal system.

810.

Rodney's commitment to public service was evident throughout his career, as he devoted himself to the cause of American independence and the well-being of his fellow citizens.

811.

During the Revolutionary War, Rodney helped organize and supply troops and provided critical support to General George Washington's Continental Army.

812.

He played a key role in securing Delaware's support for the ratification of the United States Constitution in 1787.

813.

Rodney's political ideology aligned with the Democratic-Republican Party, which opposed a strong central government and favored states' rights.

814.

In 1789, Rodney was elected as the first Governor of Delaware under the new Constitution, serving in that capacity until his death.

815.

Rodney was known for his staunch support of individual liberties and his belief in the importance of an informed and engaged citizenry.

816.

He had a reputation for being a skilled orator and persuasive speaker, using his eloquence to rally support for causes he believed in.

817.

Rodney's personal life was marked by tragedy. He never married and had no children, but he was a devoted uncle and helped raise his sister's children after her death.

818.

Rodney was a man of modest means who lived a simple and frugal lifestyle. He believed in public service as a duty rather than a means to personal gain.

819.

Despite his limited formal education, Rodney was well-read and knowledgeable about history, philosophy, and political theory.

820.

Rodney's legacy in Delaware is celebrated through various landmarks and institutions, including the Caesar Rodney Statue in Wilmington and the Caesar Rodney High School in Camden.

821.

He is also honored as one of Delaware's three representatives in the National Statuary Hall Collection in the U.S. Capitol.

822.

Rodney's contributions to the founding of the United States are recognized and commemorated by historians and scholars.

823.

He was a proponent of religious freedom and played a role in the establishment of the Delaware Constitution, which guaranteed religious liberty to all citizens.

824.

Rodney's decision to ride through the night to cast his vote for independence demonstrated his unwavering commitment to the cause of liberty and his willingness to sacrifice for it.

825.

He was known for his strong sense of duty and honor, always putting
the needs of his country and fellow citizens above his own.   .

826.

Rodney's physical appearance, with his distinctive facial cancer,
made him a memorable figure, symbolizing his resilience and
determination in the face of adversity.

827.

Rodney's service to Delaware extended beyond politics. He also
worked to improve the state's infrastructure, advocating for the
construction of roads and bridges.

828.

In addition to his political and legal career, Rodney was a successful
farmer and landowner, actively managing his properties and
contributing to Delaware's agricultural industry.

829.

Rodney's commitment to public service and his belief in democratic
principles earned him the respect and admiration of his peers.

830.

He was known for his humility and approachability, often engaging
in discussions with ordinary citizens and seeking their input on
important issues.

831.

Rodney's leadership and political acumen helped establish Delaware
as an influential state in early American politics.

832.

He was a firm believer in the importance of a strong central
government and the need for unity among the states.

833.

Rodney's efforts to promote education in Delaware led to the establishment of schools and libraries, ensuring that future generations would have access to knowledge and learning.

834.

Despite facing opposition and challenges throughout his career, Rodney remained steadfast in his commitment to the principles of liberty, equality, and justice.

835.

He was a champion of the common man and worked to protect the rights and interests of everyday citizens.

836.

Rodney's legacy as a founding father of the United States continues to inspire and influence generations of Americans.

837.

He is remembered as a dedicated patriot who put the interests of his country above his own personal well-being.

838.

Rodney's impact on Delaware and the nation as a whole can be seen in the principles and values he fought for during his lifetime.

839.

His contributions to the American Revolution helped shape the course of history and laid the foundation for the democratic ideals on which the United States was built.

840.

Rodney's commitment to public service and his unwavering belief in the principles of freedom and equality continue to resonate with people today.

841.

His courage in the face of adversity and his willingness to make personal sacrifices for the greater good serve as an inspiration to future generations.

842.

Rodney's reputation as an honest and principled politician remains intact, making him a role model for those seeking to serve their communities and uphold democratic values.

843.

He believed in the power of reason and dialogue, advocating for peaceful resolutions to conflicts and promoting civil discourse among political rivals.

844.

Rodney's ability to bridge divides and find common ground earned him the respect and admiration of his colleagues, regardless of their political affiliations.

845.

His commitment to justice extended to the legal system, where he fought for fair and impartial courts and advocated for the rights of the accused.

846.

Rodney's influence on Delaware's early history is evident in the state's commitment to preserving its democratic institutions and promoting civic engagement.

847.

He played a significant role in shaping Delaware's constitution and legal framework, ensuring that the state would be governed by principles of fairness and equality.

848.

Rodney's dedication to public service was recognized and appreciated by his fellow citizens, who often sought his guidance and leadership in times of crisis.

849.

His legacy as a founding father and statesman is celebrated not only in Delaware but also across the United States, where his contributions to the nation's early years are widely acknowledged.

850.

Rodney's life and achievements remind us of the importance of individuals who are willing to stand up for what they believe in and fight for the principles that define a nation.

851.

George Ross was a lawyer, judge, and signer of the United States Declaration of Independence.

852.

He was born on May 10, 1730, in New Castle, Delaware, to a prominent family of Scottish descent.

853.

Ross studied law and was admitted to the bar in 1750, establishing a successful legal practice in Lancaster, Pennsylvania.

854.

He was known for his keen intellect, persuasive speaking skills, and deep knowledge of the law.

855.

Ross served as a judge in Pennsylvania's Court of Common Pleas and later as a member of the provincial assembly.

856.

In 1774, Ross was elected to the Continental Congress, where he became a vocal advocate for American independence.

857.

He was a respected and influential member of Congress, known for his measured approach and ability to build consensus among his colleagues.

858.

Ross played a significant role in the drafting and adoption of the Declaration of Independence, signing the document on August 2, 1776.

859.

As a delegate from Pennsylvania, Ross represented the interests of his state and worked towards forging a united front in the fight for independence.

860.

Ross was actively involved in the Revolutionary War effort, serving on various committees and supporting the Continental Army.

861.

He was a strong proponent of establishing a strong central government and played a key role in the development of the Articles of Confederation.

862.

Ross was an advocate for religious freedom and supported the separation of church and state, believing in the importance of individual liberties.

863.

He was known for his integrity and fairness as a judge, earning the respect and trust of his colleagues and constituents.

864.

Ross had a reputation for being approachable and compassionate, often providing legal aid to those who could not afford representation.

865.

He was committed to the principles of democracy and believed in the power of an informed citizenry to shape the future of the nation.

866.

Ross was deeply invested in the welfare of his community and played a role in various civic and charitable organizations.

867.

Despite his dedication to public service, Ross experienced financial challenges throughout his life, including difficulties with debt.

868.

Ross was a staunch supporter of the rights of property owners and worked to protect individual property rights in the face of British encroachments.

869.

He played a key role in drafting Pennsylvania's state constitution and served as its vice president from 1777 to 1778.

870.

Ross's legal expertise and knowledge of British law made him a valuable asset in the legal battles against British tyranny.

871.

He had a close working relationship with other prominent figures of the American Revolution, including Benjamin Franklin and John Dickinson.

872.

Ross's signature on the Declaration of Independence is distinctive, with a flourish that sets it apart from other signatories.

873.

After his time in Congress, Ross returned to his legal practice and continued to serve the public in various capacities.

874.

He was appointed as a judge of the Pennsylvania Supreme Court and later served as vice president of the Delaware state convention that ratified the U.S. Constitution.

875.

Ross's contributions to the establishment of the United States were recognized and celebrated by his peers and fellow citizens.

876.

He was known for his strong work ethic and dedication to upholding the principles of justice and equality.

877.

Ross's commitment to the cause of independence never wavered, even in the face of personal and financial hardships.

878.

He believed in the importance of representative government and the rights of citizens to participate in the political process.

879.

Ross's legal expertise and knowledge of constitutional law were instrumental in shaping the new nation's legal framework.

880.

He played a key role in the development of Pennsylvania's legal system, helping to establish precedents and procedures that continue to guide the state's courts.

881.

Ross's legacy as a founding father of the United States is honored in various ways, including statues, memorials, and historical markers.

882.

His contributions to the establishment of the nation are remembered and celebrated on Independence Day and throughout the year.

883.

Ross's life and achievements serve as an inspiration to future generations, reminding us of the importance of dedication, integrity, and a commitment to the principles of liberty and justice.

884.

He was a respected member of the legal community, known for his deep knowledge of the law and his ability to argue cases persuasively.

885.

Ross's dedication to public service extended beyond his political career, as he continued to serve as a trusted legal advisor to individuals and organizations in need.

886.

He believed in the power of education and was a strong advocate for the establishment of schools and the promotion of knowledge and learning.

887.

Ross was a devoted family man, with a loving wife and children who supported him in his pursuits.

888.

He was known for his sharp wit and sense of humor, often using it to diffuse tension and bring people together.

889.

Ross's commitment to the principles of democracy and individual rights made him a champion for marginalized communities, including enslaved African Americans and Native Americans.

890.

He played a role in the abolitionist movement, advocating for the end of slavery and working towards a more just and inclusive society.

891.

Ross's contributions to the early years of the United States helped shape the nation's identity and laid the foundation for the democratic ideals we hold today.

892.

He believed in the power of compromise and sought common ground among competing factions, recognizing the importance of unity in achieving collective goals.

893.

Ross's leadership and diplomatic skills were instrumental in fostering collaboration and cooperation among the states during the nation's formative years.

894.

He was a strong advocate for economic independence and worked towards the development of domestic industries to reduce reliance on foreign imports.

895.

Ross's commitment to public service and his unwavering belief in the principles of freedom and equality continue to inspire and guide us today.

896.

He believed in the importance of civic engagement and encouraged citizens to participate actively in the political process.

897.

Ross's legacy extends beyond his political and legal accomplishments, as he left an indelible mark on the communities he served and the lives he touched.

898.

He was a man of integrity and principle, known for his honesty and ethical conduct in all aspects of his life.

899.

Ross's contributions to the American Revolution and the establishment of the United States are recognized and celebrated by historians and scholars.

900.

His life and achievements serve as a reminder of the extraordinary individuals who risked their lives and fortunes for the cause of freedom and the pursuit of a more perfect union.

901.

The blacktip reef shark (Carcharhinus melanopterus) is a species of requiem shark found in shallow, tropical coral reef habitats.

902.

They are named after the distinctive black tips on their fins, particularly the first dorsal fin and the caudal fin.

903.

These sharks are relatively small, typically reaching lengths of 4 to 5 feet (1.2 to 1.5 meters) and weighing around 40 to 50 pounds (18 to 23 kilograms).

904.

Blacktip reef sharks have a slender body with a streamlined shape, allowing them to move swiftly through the water.

905.

They have a gray to brownish-gray coloration on their upper body, fading to a white underside.

906.

Their diet mainly consists of small reef fish, crustaceans, and cephalopods.

907.

Blacktip reef sharks are highly adaptable and can tolerate a wide range of salinities, allowing them to move between different habitats.

908.

These sharks are known for their acrobatic displays, often leaping out of the water, particularly when chasing prey.

909.

They are typically solitary animals, but can occasionally be found in small groups or aggregations.

910.

Blacktip reef sharks have a lifespan of around 10 to 15 years in the wild.

911.

They are highly territorial and will defend their preferred area of the reef against intruders.

912.

These sharks have a unique reproductive strategy known as viviparity, where the embryos develop inside the mother's body and are nourished by a placental connection.

913.

The gestation period of blacktip reef sharks is around 10 to 12 months, with females giving birth to 2 to 4 live pups.

914.

Young blacktip reef sharks are born with fully functional teeth and are capable of hunting shortly after birth.

915.

They have a high metabolism and require a constant intake of food to meet their energy needs.

916.

Blacktip reef sharks are known for their keen sense of smell, which helps them locate prey in the water.

917.

They have small, serrated teeth that are designed for grasping and tearing prey.

918.

These sharks are not considered a significant threat to humans and are generally shy and non-aggressive.

919.

However, caution should be exercised when swimming in areas where blacktip reef sharks are present, as they may become defensive if provoked.

920.

Blacktip reef sharks are an important part of the coral reef ecosystem, helping to maintain the balance of fish populations and contributing to overall reef health.

921.

They are known to play a role in controlling the population of smaller reef fish, which helps to prevent overgrazing of coral and algae.

922.

Blacktip reef sharks have adapted to hunting in shallow water and are often seen patrolling the edges of coral reefs in search of prey.

923.

They have a unique hunting technique called "tailing," where they swim with their dorsal fin exposed above the water, allowing them to surprise their prey from below.

924.

These sharks are capable of quick bursts of speed, reaching speeds of up to 20 miles per hour (32 kilometers per hour).

925.

Blacktip reef sharks have a specialized respiratory system that allows them to extract oxygen from the water efficiently, enabling them to remain active for extended periods.

926.

They have a lateral line system, a series of sensory organs along their sides that detect changes in water pressure and movement, helping them locate prey and navigate their environment.

927.

These sharks are known to engage in social behaviors such as courtship rituals and mating displays.

928.

They have been observed engaging in "nosing," a behavior where two sharks swim alongside each other, rubbing their bodies together.

929.

Blacktip reef sharks are not migratory, but they may move between different parts of the reef in response to changing environmental conditions or the availability of food.

930.

They have a low reproductive rate, with females typically producing offspring every two to three years.

931.

Blacktip reef sharks are vulnerable to overfishing, habitat degradation, and other human impacts on coral reef ecosystems.

932.

Conservation efforts are underway to protect these sharks and their habitats, including the establishment of marine protected areas.

933.

They are classified as near-threatened by the International Union for Conservation of Nature (IUCN).

934.

Blacktip reef sharks are popular attractions in shark diving and snorkeling experiences, where tourists can observe them in their natural habitat.

935.

They are known for their graceful swimming style and elegant movements underwater.

936.

Blacktip reef sharks have a complex social hierarchy within their populations, with dominant individuals asserting their dominance over subordinate sharks.

937.

They have been studied for their role in the transmission of diseases and parasites within coral reef ecosystems.

938.

These sharks have a strong immune system, which helps them resist infections and diseases.

939.

They are sensitive to changes in water temperature and quality, making them important indicators of the overall health of coral reefs.

940.

Blacktip reef sharks have been known to exhibit curiosity towards human divers, often approaching them closely to investigate.

941.

They have a keen sense of hearing and can detect low-frequency sounds, including the movements of potential prey.

942.

These sharks are capable of jumping out of the water to catch birds or other small animals that may be flying near the surface.

943.

They have a unique pattern of black markings on their body, which provides camouflage in the dappled light of the reef.

944.

Blacktip reef sharks have been known to form temporary hunting alliances with other shark species, such as gray reef sharks or whitetip reef sharks, to improve their hunting success.

945.

They have a flexible diet and can adapt to changes in prey availability, allowing them to survive in different reef ecosystems.

946.

Blacktip reef sharks are capable of sensing changes in the Earth's magnetic field, which helps them navigate during long-distance migrations.

947.

They have a specialized organ called the ampullae of Lorenzini, which allows them to detect weak electrical signals given off by their prey.

948.

These sharks have a unique reproductive behavior known as "embryonic diapause," where the development of embryos can be delayed until environmental conditions are favorable.

949.

Blacktip reef sharks are known to have a close association with cleaner fish, allowing them to benefit from parasite removal and grooming services.

950.

They have a strong homing instinct and will often return to the same areas of the reef year after year.

951.

The blacktip shark (Carcharhinus limbatus) is a species of requiem shark known for its distinctive black-tipped fins.

952.

They are found in warm coastal waters around the world, including the Atlantic Ocean, Indian Ocean, and Pacific Ocean.

953.

Blacktip sharks are medium-sized, typically reaching lengths of 5 to 6 feet (1.5 to 1.8 meters) and weighing around 40 to 60 pounds (18 to 27 kilograms).

954.

Their name comes from the prominent black tips on their dorsal fin, pectoral fins, and lower caudal fin.

955.

They have a sleek, streamlined body with a gray to bronze-colored upper body and a white underside.

956.

Blacktip sharks are highly adapted for speed and agility, allowing them to pursue fast-swimming prey.

957.

Their diet consists mainly of small fish, including sardines, herring, and anchovies, as well as crustaceans.

958.

These sharks are known for their acrobatic displays, often leaping out of the water while hunting or when they are startled.

959.

Blacktip sharks are capable of swimming at high speeds, reaching bursts of up to 20 miles per hour (32 kilometers per hour).

960.

They have a lifespan of around 12 to 15 years in the wild.

961.

These sharks are highly migratory and can cover long distances in search of food and suitable breeding grounds.

962.

Blacktip sharks are known to form large aggregations during migration and breeding seasons.

963.

They have a unique reproductive strategy called viviparity, where the embryos develop inside the mother's body and are nourished by a placental connection.

964.

The gestation period for blacktip sharks is around 10 to 12 months, and females give birth to 4 to 7 live pups.

965.

Newborn blacktip sharks are around 20 to 30 inches (50 to 75 centimeters) in length.

966.

They have a keen sense of smell and can detect the scent of prey from a considerable distance.

967.

Blacktip sharks have specialized electroreceptors called ampullae of Lorenzini, which allow them to sense the electrical fields produced by their prey.

968.

These sharks are not considered a significant threat to humans and are generally shy and non-aggressive.

969.

However, caution should be exercised when swimming in areas where blacktip sharks are present.

970.

They are important predators in coastal ecosystems, helping to maintain the balance of fish populations and contributing to overall ecosystem health.

971.

They are important predators in coastal ecosystems, helping to maintain the balance of fish populations and contributing to overall ecosystem health.

972.

They have a complex hierarchy within their social groups, with dominant individuals asserting their dominance over subordinate sharks.

973.

These sharks have a higher tolerance for low salinity than some other shark species, allowing them to inhabit estuarine and brackish waters.

974.

Blacktip sharks have been observed engaging in courtship displays, where males will chase and bite the female's pectoral fins.

975.

They have a keen sense of hearing and can detect low-frequency sounds, including the movements of potential prey.

976.

Blacktip sharks have relatively small, serrated teeth that are well-suited for grasping and tearing apart their prey.

977.

They have a complex hunting technique that involves stalking, ambushing, and rapid acceleration to capture their prey.

978.

These sharks play an essential role in the ecosystem by controlling populations of smaller fish and maintaining the health of coral reefs and seagrass beds.

979.

They are known to associate with other shark species, such as spinner sharks and lemon sharks, during feeding activities.

980.

Blacktip sharks have been observed engaging in group feeding behaviors, where they encircle schools of fish and drive them towards the surface.

981.

They have a unique respiratory system that allows them to extract oxygen efficiently from the water, enabling them to remain active and agile.

982.

Blacktip sharks have an incredible ability to heal wounds quickly, with studies showing that their wounds can close within hours or days.

983.

They are vulnerable to overfishing, primarily due to their valuable fins, which are highly sought after for shark fin soup.

984.

Conservation efforts are in place to protect blacktip sharks, including fishing regulations and the establishment of marine protected areas.

985.

They are listed as near-threatened by the International Union for Conservation of Nature (IUCN) due to population declines caused by overfishing and habitat degradation.

986.

Blacktip sharks have been studied for their navigational abilities, with research suggesting that they use a combination of magnetic fields, visual cues, and chemical signals to navigate.

987.

They have a unique hunting strategy called "spy-hopping," where they raise their heads above the water surface to observe potential prey.

988.

Blacktip sharks are known to engage in courtship rituals, including biting and chasing behavior, to attract mates.

989.

They have a high tolerance for varying water temperatures and can adapt to different thermal conditions.

990.

These sharks have a unique pattern of dark spots on their bodies, which helps them blend in with their surroundings and provides camouflage.

991.

Blacktip sharks have been observed engaging in feeding frenzies, where multiple sharks converge on a concentrated food source.

992.

They are capable of jumping out of the water to catch prey, such as small fish or seabirds, that are near the water's surface.

993.

These sharks have a complex nervous system, allowing them to process and respond to sensory information quickly.

994.

Blacktip sharks have a strong immune system, which helps them resist infections and diseases.

995.

They are capable of regenerating damaged or lost teeth, with new teeth continuously growing to replace old ones.

996.

These sharks play a crucial role in the cultural and economic value of shark tourism, as they are popular attractions for divers and snorkelers.

997.

They have been studied for their role in the transmission of diseases and parasites within marine ecosystems.

998.

Blacktip sharks have a unique way of conserving energy while swimming, known as "ram ventilation," where they force water through their gills by swimming with their mouths open.

999.

They are known for their elegant and graceful swimming style, with smooth and fluid movements.

1000.

Blacktip sharks have a strong homing instinct and will often return to the same areas year after year, particularly during breeding and feeding seasons.